From Bad Grades to a

Great Life!

*Unlocking the
Mystery of Achievement
for Your Child*

Dr. Charles Fay

From Bad Grades to a
Great Life!

*Unlocking the
Mystery of Achievement
for Your Child*

Dr. Charles Fay

 Love and Logic

Based on a series of popular
Love and Logic Journal articles by Dr. Fay.

Love and Logic Institute, Inc.
2207 Jackson St
Golden, CO 80401
www.loveandlogic.com
800-338-4065

Love and Logic, Love & Logic, Becoming a Love and Logic Parent, America's Parenting Experts, Love and Logic Magic, 9 Essential Skills for the Love and Logic Classroom, Parenting with Love and Logic, Love and Logic Early Childhood Parenting Made Fun!, Early Childhood Parenting Made Fun! and ⓒ are registered trademarks or trademarks of the Institute For Professional Development, Ltd. and may not be used without written permission expressly granted from the Institute For Professional Development, Ltd.

ISBN# 978-1-935326-08-3

Library of Congress Cataloging-in-Publication Data

Fay, Charles, 1964-
   From bad grades to a great life! unlocking the mystery of achievement for your child / Dr. Charles Fay.
      p. cm.
   ISBN 978-1-935326-08-3
1. Education--Parent participation. 2. Academic achievement. 3. Child rearing. I. Title.
   LB1048.5.F39 2011
   649'.1--dc23
                            2011024592

Cover & Book Design: Michael Snell, Shade of the Cottonwood, L.L.C., Lawrence, KS
Project Coordinator: Kelly Borden

 Published and printed in the United States of America

Contents

Acknowledgments

To my Lord and Savior Jesus Christ: You have comforted and strengthened me through my darkest days. You have given me a wonderful wife and children. You have guided me, nurtured me, loved me, and disciplined me. You have healed my weakened body of cancer and given happiness and hope for eternity. I pray that I may bless others as your ever present love has blessed me.

To my wife, Monica: You are beautiful inside and out! Thank you for your patience, your love, and your wonderful example.

To my parents, Jim and Shirley Fay: Thank you for loving me and always seeing the very best in me. You have always encouraged me to follow my gifts, and I thank God for you every day.

Your Underachiever Can Have a Great Life!

Your underachiever really can have a great life! Why am I so sure? Two reasons: The first has to do with my professional experience over the past twenty-some years...my observations of countless academically apathetic kids who've grown to become respectful, responsible, and successful adults. The second has to do with my personal experience. As a child I was a legendary underachiever. The only motivation I had in the classroom involved trying to figure out how to avoid doing my work by making countless treks to the pencil sharpener, threatening that I'd wet my pants if I didn't receive yet another bathroom break, or getting sent to the principal's office for getting on my teacher's last nerve.

Now the cat's out of the proverbial bag. How ironic! You're reading a book about motivating kids...written by an underachiever.

To set the record straight, I eventually developed an intense love of learning and earned a real Ph.D. diploma from a reputable major American university. Nope, it's not the type you send away for by filling out a form in the back of a magazine and including $9.95, plus shipping and handling. Since that time, I've devoted myself to understanding the art and science behind upping the odds of raising respectful, responsible, and successful kids.

It wasn't long before what I was learning by studying books, pouring over research, and working with real-life kids began to coincide with what I learned in the fourth grade:

> ### *Punishing kids for failing to learn*
> ### *doesn't make them love learning.*

I knew that when I was nine! As a mere youngster I also felt that most of the things my parents and teachers were doing in order to motivate me just made me feel more and more disgusted with school. As a Ph.D. psychologist I soon noticed that these same techniques had equally dismal results with the children I was trying to motivate. Listed below are just a few of the things I've learned the hard way:

- When I lectured and reminded kids to do their work, it just made them "forget" to do it more frequently.
- When I punished them for not doing their work, most of them just got more stubborn.
- When I tried to reward them for doing their work, they'd do it… but only if I gave them a good enough treat.
- The harder I worked to make kids learn, the less they did.
- Even whining and begging didn't work.

Then it hit me! If I'd just listened to the nine-year-old inside I would have saved myself…and many of my clients…a lot of grief. Even as an underachieving kid I knew the truth about making kids learn:

You can't do it. Only they can.

One cold winter morning I had an appointment with a DC-10 headed to the Upper Midwest. This meant that I had to leave my home in the mountains of Colorado by 5:00 a.m. sharp. This, in turn, meant that I was scurrying around the house at 4:55 a.m., trying to get ready. This, in turn, also resulted in frantically heading out the door carrying my briefcase, a cup of coffee, a bagel, a rat's nest of important papers, and my carry-on suitcase. As I neared the car, a sickening sensation hit me: I'd just stepped on the slipperiest piece of ice in the driveway and gravity was sucking me to the earth's surface. In desperation I grabbed for the door handle of my car, managing to remain upright rather than embracing the pavement.

Although the dog was enjoying my bagel, my papers were blowin' in the wind, and my pants were a wonderful hue of mocha, I'd kept myself upright.

So…you may be wondering…what does slipping on the ice have to do with your underachieving kid?

Simply put, the answer has to do with the fact that the human brain filters out all information that is not directly relevant to immediate survival. As I felt myself falling, what existed in my mind? Nothing but the door handle. At that precise moment in time, the only thing existing on earth was that car part…that simple little automotive appendage representing survival in a cold and very slippery world.

Over the past two decades I've come to realize that underachieving kids are almost always slipping on the ice. That is, they're almost always preoccupied by a variety of concerns that take precedence over learning and achievement. In other words, their subconscious minds are so concerned with emotional…and sometimes physical… needs that they have no energy or attention left over for learning.

I've also learned that this doesn't only apply to kids growing up in dysfunctional families, chaotic neighborhoods, or poverty. Plenty come from nice families, with nice incomes and nice values. The common denominator, though, is that the adults in their lives have fallen into the trap of thinking that simply providing more consequences or rewards will solve the problem. The adults in their lives are overlooking the fact that motivation to learn comes from internal curiosity…rather than external coercion.

> ***Motivation to learn comes from internal curiosity…
> rather than external coercion.***

Before we get much further, it's probably good for you to know that I've become a pretty old-fashioned sort of guy. I didn't used to be so old-fashioned until I learned the hard way that most of the new-fashioned ideas I was hearing weren't working so hot for folks. Anyway, I've learned to be old-fashioned. Thus, every fiber of my soul believes that people should be held accountable for their actions. Because of this, I think consequences can be a very necessary and useful tool. They seem to work great when kids have misbehaved or have caused some sort of problem for other people. Unfortunately, they don't seem to work so well when kids are struggling with unmet needs and are feeling so hopeless that they don't care. In other words, consequences don't seem to work so great when people are causing problems for themselves.

When a child is not learning, who are they really causing a problem for? Themselves!

Rewards seem to work pretty well, too. That is as long as they are used sparingly and a child is not dealing with unmet needs for emotional or physical survival. Sadly, when the only thing that kids can think about is trying to meet needs for competence, control, affection, belonging, etc., even the greatest rewards have only temporary results.

This book is all about meeting the deepest of our children's needs. When this happens, their brains are freed up to think about reading, writing, arithmetic, and other academic subjects.

> *Time and time again, I see children blossom from the inside-out when the adults in their lives help them feel better from the inside-out.*

This book is also all about raising kids with great character. At the Love and Logic Institute we believe that developing character (i.e. learning to be polite, honest, caring, industrious, etc.) is far more important than getting good grades.

What's the most spectacularly glorious part? When we focus on character we also meet basic needs for competence, affection, control, and inclusion. In essence, we up the odds that our children's brains will be relaxed enough to enjoy learning.

I chose the title of this book after a massive amount of reflection on what I believe to be most important for helping children develop the skills necessary for a great life. The title *From Bad Grades to a Great Life!* means to me that that there is hope for all kids. It means that some will have a great life because their parents focus on character and their grades get better over time. It also means that some will enjoy a great life because their parents focus on character, their grades never improve very much, but their character leads them to great success in less academic occupations. The underlying theme… the anchor…the cornerstone…is placing our focus on raising kids who become great people.

> *Great people...regardless of their*
> *academic achievements...*
> *seem to find some way to have*
> *great lives.*

The subtitle was also chosen with great care. The title *Unlocking the Mystery of Achievement for Your Child* means to me that this book focuses on the underlying, often "mysterious" aspects of motivation and achievement. These aspects are "mysterious" because our society has gradually ignored lasting solutions in favor of quick fixes. The things that create great human beings are those things that take time and often seem unrelated to your seventh grader getting better grades in her science class. They seem mysterious because our modern world has relegated being a good person to a much lowlier position than making tons of money, driving an expensive car, and owning a house with at least four toilets. They seem mysterious because they involve deeper attitudes and values about life, instead of surface issues, such as the fact that *i* comes before *e* except after *c* and $a2 + b2 = c2$.

This book is only for those folks who've already realized that they can't make their kids learn. This book is also for those of you who realize that there is much more to attaining success in life than getting good grades. This book is only for those who want to raise kids who become the nicest, most honest, most conscientious, and most responsible citizens on their blocks.

If you like vague, theoretical books, return this one. My goal is to give you *things that you can do*...not just things that you can think about. To this end I've included numerous text boxes with the heading **"Love and Logic Experiment."** Each of these represents a practical suggestion for helping your child develop the skills essential for enjoying a great life. Most of these also up the odds that they'll also get better grades! Please don't feel like you have to do *all* of these experiments!

Experiment with only one or two
Love and Logic Experiments at a time.

I hope you enjoy reading this book as much as I've enjoyed writing it! I also pray that your children will develop the greatness of character required to lead a great life regardless of how high or low their grades end up being!

Are We Focusing on the Right Things?

What's more important? Getting great grades or becoming a great person?

"Underachiever"

I hear that word a lot these days. Just about everywhere I go someone is talking about the underachiever they know. Sometimes the underachiever is a son or daughter. Other times the underachiever is a student. Sometimes the underachiever is the neighbor's kid. I'm even told of underachieving spouses!

So...what should we do about these motivationally challenged folks?

In graduate school...during one of my brief breaks from being one of them...I read quite a lot of research on the subject of problem-solving. From the work of these high-achieving researchers, I learned that the most common barrier to effective problem-solving is failing to correctly define the problem. In other words, when problem-solving goes awry, it's typically because we've solved something other than the real problem. In our desperate attempts to cure the curse of underachievement, is it possible that we've been doing some damage by falling into this trap?

What is "underachievement"?

If we're going to help the underachievers in our lives, it makes sense that we get a really good handle on what this label means in the first place. And to do this, it makes sense that we should first define the opposite...achievement or success. Obviously, this is where things get muddy and all mucked up with personal ideology. My definition of success may differ from yours. It's entirely possible that you might even consider me an underachiever after reading it.

A successful person...

• Treats others with great respect and fairness.
• Loves their family and takes good care of them.
• Has the skills to gain and maintain employment and financial responsibility.
• Builds people up, rather than tearing them down.
• Serves others instead of demanding to be served.
• Takes more pride in doing good things than getting good things.

Are we ignoring the right things?

April has an IQ of 125. That's well above average. Because she has plenty of brains, everyone in April's life expects her to produce plenty of A's. There's just one problem...April is okay with B's...and sometimes C's. Oh, the horror! For years just about every adult in April's life has lamented over her lack of motivation. Many a note from school has read, "April is a joy to have in class, but she isn't performing up to her potential."

Yes, April is sweet and respectful most of the time. Sure, she's good about helping out around the house. Yep, she gets along well with other kids. Yeah, she likes to volunteer in the nursery at church. But...she isn't performing up to her potential! Dog-gone-it, April! Show us the money! Where are those big brain grades?

This sad story plays itself out in home after home around the world. With her 125 IQ, my guess is that April is well aware that she doesn't measure up in the eyes of the most important adults in her life. Because they're all so obsessed with her "underachievement," they're missing how successful she really is. Our world needs more April-like people...people who set priorities and understand that family, friends, and service are more important than income or status. Maybe the government wouldn't need to bail out so many financial institutions or big businesses if these were run by the Aprils of the world. I'm pretty sure that April would not fly to Washington, D.C. in her corporate jet to ask for a taxpayer-funded bailout.

Are we focusing on the wrong things?

Carson also has a 125 IQ. From a very early age, he found it simple and very rewarding to provide the adults in his life an ample supply of A grades. Feeling so great about these achievements, the adults in his life began to supply him with a cornucopia of accolades: "Carson, you are so bright! Carson, you are so special! Carson, you can be anything you want to be!" Since he is so very special, the adults in his life have also given him a "get out of jail free" card. He can do no wrong!

Being officially certified as bright, special, and able to do anything, Carson has chosen to do just that. Because he believes that chores are the plight of the common class, he considers himself above them. Respect is something he provides only to those he views as his equals. Some day he may meet such a person. The world is his servant.

Sure, Carson's parents and teachers see his blossoming narcissism. Sure, he treats others a bit like barnyard waste. Yep, we know that he's turned into a jerk...but his grades are awesome! Besides, he's gifted. Someday he's going to be a CEO...or a doctor...or maybe even the president!

Here's the really sad part: Parents and educators rarely ask me what to do with the Carsons of the world. It's almost as if their great grades blind us to their underlying...and very serious...underachievement. I've known many Carsons in my lifetime. Because they feel so entitled, some have left their faithful wives for younger, more exciting ones. Others have experienced no remorse as they cheated their way up the corporate ladder. One I know approached his elderly parents and demanded that they give him an advance on his inheritance. Some have worked for my business...and no longer do.

Tax-Free Wealth

Although the examples of April and Carson clearly represent the extremes, this underlying dynamic is seen in practically every case of "underachievement." Far too little focus is being placed on being a good person, whereas far too much is being placed on transcripts.

In response to my stance here, many argue, "How will my child get into a good university if they don't have the best grades?" I started my higher education at a very small, unknown community college. I guess that's why I never made anything of my life.

Don't get me wrong. Academic learning is very, very important! Grades are very important! What's more important, though, is that our children first learn how to live life with compassion and character. When we give them this gift, we nearly guarantee their life-long success. Because their wealth comes from the inside-out, it will never be lost, stolen, or taxed away by the U.S. government. They will always be rich...regardless of the type of job they someday acquire.

The Foundation of Success

Something ironic often happens when we place our focus on character instead of grades: Our children's academic achievement slowly begins to improve. Why? Because successful students know how to:

- Delay gratification.
- Persevere when a task becomes boring or tedious.
- Maintain a positive attitude when they make mistakes or experience failure.
- Accept corrective feedback without becoming angry, sullen, or depressed.
- Cooperate and compromise.

Focusing on character teaches our children the core competencies required for success with academic learning. While their grades may not be as high as those "earned" by kids whose parents are micromanaging every aspect of the academic education...or by kids whose parents are doing more homework than they are...they will be far better prepared for life.

So...what can we do with our underachiever?

Listed below are just a few things we can do on a daily basis to dramatically up the odds for success. As this book unfolds in your hands, you'll see a separate chapter devoted to describing each in much greater detail:

Recognize and celebrate their gifts.

Your child has gifts! Do you know what they are? Are they aware of their gifts? Do they see that you value these gifts, as well? Do they believe that it is their job to use their gifts to help others? If the answer to any of these questions is "no" or "I'm not so sure," there's no time to waste! Far too many children lose their gifts because these strengths are never identified, valued, or allowed to mature.

Analyzing the lives of truly great people, we find they were blessed not so much with a large number of gifts...but that they were allowed to spend a massive amount of time on the ones they had. Please don't make the grave mistake of trying to motivate your child in their area of weakness by taking away their areas of strength.

Love and Logic Experiment

Start today by making a list of things your child is naturally good at. Keep this list in a place where you see it each and every day. Use this little exercise to begin a commitment to helping your child lead a life focused on the joy of their strengths rather than the frustration of their weaknesses.

Expect politeness and respect.

Is your child polite and respectful? There is nothing worse than an extremely gifted...yet arrogant...child. Kids who learn how to say "please" and "thank you" become far more successful adults than those who don't. Children who learn how to remain respectful when they don't get their way will enjoy a huge advantage in life.

Love and Logic Experiment

Start today by saying this to your child: "I do things for people who say 'please' and 'thank you.'" In a very polite and respectful way provide what they want only when they can use these two magic words. Expect them to get pretty annoyed in the short-term and more fun-to-be-around in the long-term.

Expect them to complete their fair share of family chores.
Chores represent a key portion of the foundation required for lifelong success! Are your children completing them without reminders and without pay? If not, they're missing out on vital opportunities to learn responsibility and to feel like loved and needed members of the family. When they learn how to do chores without a battle, the odds go way up that they'll also learn to complete their schoolwork without a battle.

Love and Logic Experiment

Start today by creating a nice little sign for your refrigerator:

In our family, we help each other because we love each other.

Model this by helping your child with their chores and saying, "I love you, and that's why I want to help you with this. I'll help as long as you're working harder than I am."

This represents a slow and manageable first step toward teaching your kids to do their fair share around the house. If you can't stand the suspense, skip to chapter four and learn how to respond to a stubborn young'un who says things like, "I'm not doing that! I wasn't born into this family to be a slave!"

Allow them to do without some of the things they want.

Does your child have too much stuff? If they do, they're at risk for coming to believe that there is no need to work in school...or beyond. Few things damage a child more than growing to believe that they are entitled to everything they want...without having to exert any perspiration. In contrast, kids who grow up without some of the things they want are much more likely to learn that hard work is necessary and rewarding.

Love and Logic Experiment

A great time to start is during your next trip to the store. When your child asks for something, reply, "You may have that when you can afford it." Chances are, your child won't thank you...until they are thirty and don't have a pile of debt.

Another great place to start involves saying "no" to yourself when you have that urge to buy your child something really nifty. Experiment with saying to yourself, "He's going to appreciate this so much more... and feel so much better about himself...if he has to earn this."

Create a duller home so that school seems more exciting.

Have you ever noticed that work isn't always fun? Have you ever noticed that it can even be boring at times? Kids who never experience boredom find themselves very poorly prepared for success at school and in life. If our children come to believe that life is always exciting and entertaining, how will they remain motivated when this is not the case?

Love and Logic Experiment

A great place to start involves carving out some time this weekend for your kids to get really, really bored. Sometimes this involves just hanging around the house without running around town, sometimes this involves unplugging the TV and the computers, other times this requires taking them some place like the plumbing supply store. Regardless of the specifics, we can be pretty sure that we aren't doing our job as parents if our kids are not complaining about being bored. When they do, experiment with saying, "That's too bad. I have some chores that I think might help you with that."

Let them struggle.

Has your child ever tasted the sweet success that comes from working through something really tough? Does your child believe that she has what it takes to overcome adversity? Far too many youngsters truly believe that when the going gets tough, they should give up on going.

Why has this become so common? Out of great love, far too many parents steal from their kids. They do this by doing just about everything for them. They do this by never allowing them to struggle with difficult tasks and seeing that they can succeed with effort.

Love and Logic Experiment

A smart place to start involves resisting the urge to jump in the next time you see your child getting frustrated with something. Instead, show them that you care by empathizing, "That looks like it must be really frustrating." The second step involves giving them some ideas AND allowing them to decide whether they will use them or not. The key requires that we give some quick ideas: "Some kids decide to" and then back out of the picture by saying, "Good luck, I just know that you're the kind of kid who can figure this out."

Time and time again we see children growing in self-esteem when their parents apply this simple idea. Time and time again we see that their kids eventually figure out how to overcome their challenges. Time and time again we witness how good their kids feel about their abilities when they are allowed to struggle. Are you doing too much for your kids, instead of allowing them to grapple with life's little dilemmas?

Help them develop a sense of purpose.

Your child is important! Your child can make a major difference in the world! We are relying on your child to do this! While this sounds like too much pressure to place on anyone, the truth is that human beings are wired to need a purpose in life. They're wired to be needed. Children who grow up believing that their purpose is only to serve themselves, soon become disappointed and very, very frustrated. Those who mature to believe that their purpose is to serve others discover the intense satisfaction and excitement that comes from making the world a better place. From this excited sense of purpose comes motivation to work hard.

Making the world a better place doesn't mean that your child needs to discover a cure for cancer, a clean and renewable source of energy, or any other solution to humanity's major challenges. It simply means that they see a connection between how they live their lives and the general welfare of others. Regardless of the occupation, people can choose to see themselves as performing a job…or doing something that helps the world. Those who select the latter are always happier, more motivated and less susceptible to burn out. The earlier our children learn this perspective, the better off everyone will be.

Love and Logic Experiment

Start with this: Begin to think out loud about your own job when your kids are within earshot. Allow them to overhear you talking about how what you do helps other people. If you are a housewife…or a househusband…allow them to overhear you talking about how gratifying it is to raise kids who will someday make the world a better place. When children overhear our sense of purpose, they are far more likely to develop their own.

Love them for who they are…not for the grades they get.

It can feel rather unfashionable in today's world to love our kids even when they do poorly in school. One mom put it well: "It's almost as if I feel like a bad mother if I don't fly off the handle and get all obsessed with what he's doing wrong."

Can you imagine how depressed and demotivated you'd feel if your spouse loved you only if you always met your earning potential?

Wise parents remember that love must come first. Without it all is lost.

Love and Logic Experiment

Start today by giving yourself permission to be sad for your child when they mess up. You don't have to be mad at them. It's far more effective to be sad for them. When they bring home bad grades, hug them and say:

I love you so much. I bet this is really hard. I will love you no matter how well or poorly you do in school. I just want to help.

Are you more likely to want and accept help from someone who's sad for you rather than mad at you?

Nothing works without the empathy.

My father, Jim Fay, was raised by a traditional "old school" dad who believed that his effectiveness as a parent increased with the volume of his voice. In fact…the truth be told…my grandfather probably was more effective with his kids when he raised his voice. That's because my father and his brothers grew up in the 1930s and 1940s when most parents handled things that way. When this approach was the cultural norm…and before children became convinced by television, music, and the internet that their parents were clueless…a stern, decibel-rich approach seemed to do the job.

Have things changed a bit since that time?

What children used to view as serious they now view as entertaining! Even when I was a child I believed that one of the worst things that could happen was seeing one of my parents or teachers become angry or frustrated. Have you noticed that many of today's children have a completely different perception? Have you noticed that so many now find it rather exciting...even entertaining...when their parents' or teachers' faces turn red and their voices go up?

Again...what used to be serious is now entertaining.

In the early 1970s, my father and his good friend and colleague, Foster W. Cline, M.D., became very concerned with the vast number of children they knew with R.D.D. (Responsibility Deficit Disorder). They also became intrigued by the large number of parents who were raising really respectful and responsible kids. "What are these more successful parents doing differently than their less successful peers?" they asked. Dedicated to finding an answer to this question, they began a careful study of available research, theory... and real flesh and blood people.

It wasn't long before they discovered the key:

> *The most successful parents...and educators...*
> *provided a strong dose of empathy BEFORE*
> *they delivered consequences.*

In other words, they expressed sadness instead of madness when their children earned bad grades or made bad decisions.

Instead of saying...

"For crying-out-loud. Look at these grades!"

The more successful parents said...

"Oh, no. I bet you feel awful about this report card. Let me know how I can help."

Instead of saying...

"That's it! No more television!"

The more successful ones said...

"This is such a bummer. I love you so much. I think one thing I can do to help is to remove the TV from your room so that you aren't tempted to watch it instead of doing your homework."

Instead of staying...

"How many times do I have to tell you to do your homework? I am sick and tired of having to remind you! You're grounded!"

The more successful ones empathized...

"Oh man. I can understand getting too busy to remember your chores. I love you too much to fight with you about getting them done. That's why I did them for you. How are you planning to pay me for my time?"

The part of this that's downright impossible to get across via paper and ink is the true message of sincere love and compassion the most successful folks conveyed. They weren't sarcastic. They weren't snippy. They weren't sassy. No! Instead they communicated to their children...or their students...that they truly loved them even though they didn't love their bad decisions.

What my father and Dr. Cline discovered was that this message of love and empathy allowed the children to spend more time being upset with their poor decisions than being upset with their parents or teachers. In other words:

Anger, frustration, lectures, and volume make the child's problem the adult's. Empathy allows the child's problem to remain the child's.

Love and Logic Experiment

To make the sometimes difficult shift from reacting with anger to reacting with empathy, make the following sign for your bathroom mirror, refrigerator, car dashboard, desk at work, or any other highly visible spot:

My children will learn responsibility from empathy and consequences… not anger and frustration.

Another Love and Logic Experiment...

It's also helpful to memorize just one empathetic statement, or sentence stem for use anytime you feel the anger, sarcasm, or frustration setting in. Examples include:

- This is so sad...
- Oh, man...
- What a bummer...
- This stinks...
- How sad...
- Dang...

Many folks report that having a quick and simple empathetic statement on the tip of their tongue helps them take hold of their emotions and respond in ways they can be proud of later on.

Another quick tip...

When you're too angry or frustrated to use empathy, give yourself permission to delay your reaction or delay the consequence. The next time this happens, experiment with saying:

I'm so angry right now that I can't think too well.
I make better decisions when I'm calm. I love you. We'll talk later.

Take good care of yourself!

Empathy is so critically important that no other Love and Logic techniques will work without it. That's why you'll see the following warning symbol strategically placed throughout the remainder of this book:

NOTHING WORKS WITHOUT THE EMPATHY.

When you see this warning, remind yourself that you don't have to be the "bad guy" when your kids blow it. Instead, you can lock in the empathy and allow your child's bad decision…or their bad grades…to be the "bad guy."

Character is the key.

Because some children have so much difficulty learning, they may always struggle with doing well in school. Does this mean that they can't have a successful life?

Joseph was not blessed with a 125 IQ. Unlike April and Carson, he struggled just to learn the basics. Many of his teachers viewed him as "intellectually deficient, mentally handicapped, or just plain retarded." Fortunately, his parents didn't. Instead, they devoted the lion's share of their time and energy to teaching him how to be respectful and responsible. When it came to his grades, they were sad for him when he didn't do so well and glad for him when he did.

As Joseph grew, he became a great friend to all who knew him. Being one of my classmates, I vividly remember how the room always brightened when he walked through the door. Now he works a simple job in our community, takes good care of his family, and remains a source of light in an often gloomy world.

Where would Joseph be if his parents had spent all of their time focusing on his poor grades? Could it really be the case that life success rests on character?

Your Child Has Gifts!

Don't make the mistake of focusing on their weaknesses, instead.

As a child I had two very different types of teachers. Both types cared deeply about kids, and both types were strongly committed to getting us excited about school and learning. One type, Teacher A, believed that her job was to help us figure out what we did wrong so that we could learn to do it right. With great love and passion, she spent each and every day observing our errors, providing "constructive criticism," and drilling us on our areas of weakness. When Teacher A walked by our desks, we knew that the odds were high that she would detect some fault in need of remediation. With love in her heart and her voice, she made sure that we got plenty of practice working on what we viewed to be the most personally painful.

The other variety of teacher, Teacher B, had a very different pedagogical perspective. Believing that it was her job to help us discover and hone our strengths, she spent each and every day observing our triumphs, helping us understand why we achieved them, and teaching us that great people build their lives around their natural gifts. When Teacher B walked by our desks, we knew that the odds were high of her detecting something we'd done well. While she also devoted some time to helping us correct our errors and weaknesses, most of her energy was devoted to helping us practice what charged our batteries the most.

- In whose classroom would you rather be?
- Which of these teachers is the most effective with academically reluctant or downright apathetic kids?
- Which of these teachers most closely personifies our nation's current approach to education?
- To which would you rather be married?

There is nothing more demotivating than receiving a constant diet of corrective feedback or "constructive criticism"! Well-meaning parents and educators who spend most of their energy doing so create kids who are unwilling to try when tasks become difficult. Despite their good intentions, such adults find themselves mired in countless unwinnable power struggles.

> *There is nothing more demotivating than receiving a constant diet of corrective feedback or "constructive criticism"!*

Too frequently we as parents fall into this trap. After our youngsters experience a full day's worth of error detection and weakness remediation, we greet them at the door with more. Don't make this mistake with your kids. Discussed below are some time-tested steps you can get started with right away.

Identify your child's healthy natural aptitudes.

In our quest to remediate weaknesses, it's not uncommon to become completely unaware of our children's natural gifts. Every child has at least one, and the best way to identify it is by observing what they enjoy doing the very most. As a young elementary school age kid, I spent most of my time tinkering with some mechanical device, reading books about sharks and dinosaurs, or writing wild fantasy stories in my Big Chief tablet. When I did these things, nothing else existed around me. All was right with the world!

The Teacher A's in my life gave my parents some bad advice: "Charlie isn't performing up to his potential in math. He needs to spend extra time each evening memorizing his multiplication tables, practicing his long division, and developing numerical fluency."

Since I was already good at tinkering, reading, and writing strange stories, these activities were replaced with multiplication facts, flash card drills, extra math worksheets, and endless battles with my mother over where decimal points are supposed to go.

My math skills failed to improve, and my attitude about learning went down the toilet. Fortunately, they abandoned Teacher A's well-intended yet doomed advice for a far more positive focus. By watching what I did well, they became committed to helping me hone my gifts. Life was good again!

Some children's gifts don't fall into what we traditionally view as being academically valuable. Examples include artistic, musical, mechanical, athletic, or social aptitudes.

These competencies are just as important! My father, Jim Fay, wasn't good at any school subjects as a child. He was good at play-ing his trombone, instead. It was this love of music, and his moth-er's encouragement to pursue it, that gave him the strength and self-esteem to face his learning difficulties. Success in nonacademic strength areas gives many children the courage required to stay in school and eventually succeed in their areas of weakness.

> *Success in nonacademic strength areas*
> *gives many children the courage required*
> *to stay in school and eventually succeed*
> *in their weakness areas.*

Love and Logic Experiment

When you make a list of your child's strengths, be careful to also include things that are not traditionally viewed as academically relevant. Some examples include sports, "hanging-out" with healthy peers, woodworking, art, learning about subjects not taught in school, taking care of pets, etc.

Apply common sense.

Obviously, some of the activities children are attracted to don't fall into the category of "healthy natural aptitudes." A child who spends all of his time watching television, playing frenetic video games, or chatting on the internet is not developing his natural, God-given talents. In chapter six, I discuss the perils of allowing your kids to spend too much time engaged in highly stimulating electronic activities. Quite simply, these activities raise our children's threshold for stimulation such that they view almost everything else, including their teachers, as boring.

Parents are wise to consider the following guidelines when determining whether an activity should be encouraged:

- The activity should require active thought rather than passive participation.
- The activity must support good character values, such as honesty, kindness, etc.
- The activity must not interfere with healthy peer and adult relationships.
- The activity shouldn't interfere with the completion of chores and other family responsibilities.
- If the activity is extremely stimulating and fast-paced, significant limits should be placed on how much time a child should be engaged in it.

Love and Logic Experiment

Don't be afraid to say "no" to television watching, computer games, and other fast-paced electronic entertainment. If your child argues with you about this, repeat "I love you too much to argue," in a calm, quiet tone of voice. Just become a broken record, and repeat this phrase. Remember: Trying to reason with an angry, upset child is about as effective as reasoning with a drunk.

NOTHING WORKS WITHOUT THE EMPATHY.

Don't fall into the trap of using strengths as carrots.

Too frequently, parents and educators attempt to use natural strengths as rewards for achievement in weakness areas. The problem this creates rears its ugly head when the child fails to perform and adults feel compelled to remove participation in gift areas as a consequence. When we fall into this trap, we take away what our children need the very most, and we up the odds of drug use and other high risk behaviors. Yes! Kids who are allowed to participate in healthy extracurricular activities are far less likely to participate in unhealthy ones.

Love and Logic Experiment

If you've already made the mistake of taking away something your child really needs to succeed, there is nothing wrong with admitting it to him:

Son, I need to apologize to you. I've been learning a lot about how to help kids do better in school, and I've realized that I made a mistake by telling you that you can't play sports unless you improve your grades. I still think grades are very, very important, but I now understand that doing what you really love is, too.

Encourage your child to charge their batteries before doing homework.

"Work before play." Wise words these are...except when it comes to academically reluctant, discouraged kids.

Love and Logic Experiment

If your child has become resistant to homework and refuses to talk with you about school, experiment with changing course:

Sweetie, I forbid you from doing your homework each afternoon...until you've charged yourself up by first doing something you're really good at. I've learned that successful people focus most of their time doing what they do well. This charges their batteries so that they have the energy to work on things that they don't find so easy. When you're all charged up we'll take a look at what you've gotten correct.

Focus on the correct answers... not the incorrect ones.

The last sentence of the previous Love and Logic Experiment included a critical clue: "When you're all charged up, we'll take a look at what you've gotten correct." With academically reluctant, resistant, or apathetic kids, it's wise for parents to spend nearly no time identifying and correcting what their children have done wrong. Instead, homework time should be spent celebrating what was done correctly...and encouraging our kids to identify why they were successful.

Love and Logic Experiment

Explain your new approach in the following way:

I've learned that the best way to help kids with schoolwork is to spend most of the time helping them see what they did correct...and helping them figure out how they got these things right. If it makes this easier for you, feel free to hide the wrong answers from me.

Are you guessing that your kids will be far more receptive to your help when you provide it in this way? Ironically, children are far more likely to work on what they've done wrong when we aren't harping on it.

Homework time should be spent celebrating what was done correctly...and encouraging our kids to identify why they were successful.

Love and Logic Experiment

At the Love and Logic Institute, we've developed a four-step strategy for helping children really see that success comes from hard work.

Step One: Catch your child doing something well.
This may include a math problem, part of a math problem, spelling a word correctly, or just about anything else.

Step Two: Describe what they did without praising.
This may sound like, "Look at problem number six. You did that correctly." It's important to resist the urge to say something like, "That's great!" or "Super."

Kids who are having problems with underachievement are so used to hearing these things that they rarely give them much weight. Instead they reason, "What does this person want from me?"

Step Three: Ask them why they were successful.
Most underachieving kids will say things like, "I don't know," or "Luck."

Step Four: Give them a verbal menu of possibilities.
Ask them, "Did you work hard? Did you keep trying? Or have you been practicing?"

Each one of these represents a healthy perspective on achievement: It's earned through effort.

Encourage your child to verbalize the option that best represents why they were successful. While the one they choose doesn't matter all that much, the fact that they are saying it with their own lips does.

By applying the four-step strategy discussed above, we achieve two things: First, we help our child come to realize that success comes from effort (hard work, perseverance, and practice) instead of luck or superior intelligence. Secondly, we make plenty of nice deposits into our mutual relationship bank account. The balance of this account represents how our children feel about themselves, about us, and about learning. Since the accounts of most underachievers are saddled with years of overdraft charges, it can take quite some time to get their attitudes about learning and school out of debt. Once this begins to happen, though, we can begin to make some small withdrawals in the form of correcting their mistakes and helping them grow in their areas of weakness.

After two or three weeks, experiment with making some withdrawals.

Please don't misunderstand. Correcting our children when they err is an important part of our job as parents. So is encouraging them to improve in their areas of academic weakness. By focusing most of our energy on their strengths and successes, however, we up the odds that they will be receptive to working on what they find difficult.

Love and Logic Experiment

After you've spent at least two weeks making deposits, experiment with making a small withdrawal by asking them to try something they've been resistant about in the past. Simply say:

I know this is difficult for you. Will you try it just for me?

Their reaction will tell you whether your check has cleared… or bounced. If their body language indicates "insufficient funds for withdrawal," step back and make more deposits. If they begin to display more cooperation, continue investing while gradually encouraging them to grow.

This approach is a lasting solution...not a quick fix.

Love and Logic techniques are not designed to make your kids behave perfectly or to coerce them into getting great grades. In fact, we aren't all that concerned about grades, and we believe that children learn important life lessons by making plenty of affordable mistakes. Our passion lies in helping kids become great people who are excited about learning...so that they're motivated to do it for the rest of their lives. When we put the horse in front of the cart, and we focus on character and the love of learning, grades and achievement eventually take care of themselves. When we expect the cart to pull the horse, we end up with an angry and frustrated horse.

When we focus on character and the love of learning, grades and achievement eventually take care of themselves.

Sometimes quick fixes look like they are working. In the realm of parenting and educational practice, there exist scores of programs designed to punish, reward, and micromanage kids into completing their papers and doing well on tests. Approaches such as these create kids who...

• Become dependent and need someone to babysit their learning.
• Only learn when they are coerced into learning.
• View learning as a chore rather than an opportunity.
• Get burned out on academics before they graduate from high school.
• Never realize their full natural potential for achievement and joy.

I was given many great gifts by my parents. One of the most magnificent was their decision to let me spend most of my time tinkering with mechanical things, reading books about what I loved, and writing stories in my Big Chief tablet. The rest of my life was profoundly affected by that one decision they made during my fifth year of elementary school. My hope is that the underachievers in your life will be so fortunate.

Looking back, I now realize how agonizingly difficult this decision must have been for my parents. In faith, they decided to trust that focusing on character and strengths would eventually result in a child with the skills necessary for enjoying a great life. While these skills took a long time to develop, our relationship improved almost immediately.

Would you like to spend less time fighting with your kids over schoolwork and more time rejoicing with them over their victories?

A woman blessed me with the following letter related to how they achieved this in their own home...with great long-term success:

Dear Charles,

This letter is about my son always loving trains from toddler stage, dropping out of high school and now being responsible for over 800+ employees for a major railroad. To me it's a story of persistence, following your passion, and that the easy way isn't always the best way. As the Love and Logic approach always indicates, the road to wisdom is always under construction. He has now obtained his associates degree and is working on his bachelor's degree because it's important to him.

From the time our son, Aaron, was a toddler he developed a love and fascination with trains. It started with a train going around the Christmas tree, playing with them as a child, and reading stories about trains. We encouraged the love of trains by taking him on train trips when special trains came into the area, such as steam locomotives. We also visited many different train museums during vacations. Little did we know that he was destined to follow that passion as a life career.

Aaron discovered a historical railroad club that was working on restoring old passenger cars to be used on specialized train trips. Each Saturday we would take him to work on those cars with the club members. He would talk with excitement about the different cars they worked on as well as the history of the car. He learned many life skills such as reworking brake systems, painting, electrical wiring, and ways to clean up old train equipment.

In school there were struggles, primarily around work completion. We sought the help of an educational psychologist as we knew that power struggles would only make matters worse. Many people believe it is a sign of weakness to ask for help, yet it is really a sign of strength and can bring clarity to the issues. The psychologist indicated that sometimes kids make mistakes and you have to love them enough to guide them through the mistakes. At 16, our son dropped out of high school. The words of the psychologist proved to be important to maintain our relationship throughout these difficult times.

Aaron had many jobs. He still had his daily paper routes with 200+ customers. He became a certified bowling mechanic and worked at a variety of bowling lanes. He continued to volunteer at the historical railroad club.

It was his love of trains and desire to work for the railroad that lead him to get his GED. After many attempts to get an interview with the railroad he was successful in getting a job working in the rail maintenance department. He worked part-time on a dinner train. He also found jobs on short line railroads to further his knowledge and skills. His goal was to get a job as an engineer for a major railroad.

His persistence and focus worked when he was hired as a conductor on a major railroad working on freight trains. His skills, knowledge, dedication, and excellent problem-solving skills provided him with the opportunity to attend training to become an engineer. Before he was 22, he completed his training as "top gun" with the highest score. His dream was realized and he continued to expand his goals.

Since that time Aaron has been promoted numerous times and is currently responsible for over 800 employees. His skill to see the "big picture" and diagnose problems helped with his advancements. Yet, he knew he needed to return to school to develop additional knowledge about management and business organizations. He has already completed his associate's degree and is currently working on finishing his bachelor's degree.

How many people do you know who are working in an area they were always passionate about? NOT MANY!!! While the path wasn't easy and required much dedication, persistence, desire, and belief that *it was possible the goal was achieved. We've learned that mistakes are wonderful learning opportunities. Aaron wished he had made different choices when he was younger, yet he is stronger as the result of those experiences.*

We didn't know about Love and Logic back then. Maybe that educational psychologist did, as much of the advice he gave us certainly follows the philosophy of Love and Logic. It is so important to make sure that you love your children unconditionally and they know it. It is also important to find out what your children's strengths and passions are. They can build on them and use them to lead them through those difficult times.

This story has been shared with many parents as they struggle with their children's academic success. It is so important to assist parents in looking at and encouraging their child's strengths. It is the best gift, since from their strengths they now have a road map of what they want to accomplish. Their goals, dedication, persistence, and resilience will take them wherever they want to go.

Gloria

Is Your Child Polite and Respectful?

If they are, they've got a head start on a great life!

These days there's lots of talk about achievement among all the high achieving folks who run our schools…and our government. As a result, every state has some sort of test to measure it. In my home state of Colorado, we call it the C.S.A.P. One of my sons thinks the acronym stands for "Causes School to be an Awful Place." While I think he overstates his case, I do believe that big tests can cause some unintended negative side-effects…like leaving kids and their teachers stressed out.

But…nevertheless…gobs of taxpayer cash and educator time is spent testing kids to see if they know what's on the test. That's not necessarily horrible, but I do worry that some schools and teachers are spending more time teaching kids what's on that test than teaching them how to think and learn. I also worry that important things…such as basic goodness of character…are getting downplayed because they aren't on the test. Maybe my concerns are valid…or maybe I have them only because I went to school back when kids were deprived of taking those sorts of really big tests.

Regardless, I still find myself fretting. I just keep worrying... worrying that maybe excellence in reading, writing, and arithmetic isn't enough for success in life. I bite my nails over the number of kids...and adults...who don't understand that great academic success still won't help you keep a job if you act like a jerk. I keep wondering:

> ***With this big push for academic accountability***
> ***in the schools, have some lost sight of***
> ***equally important character characteristics such as***
> ***politeness and respect?***

Maybe I'm nuts, but it seems like polite and respectful kids enjoy a number of lifelong advantages. For starters, they get far more kudos from their teachers. Why? Because they give far more kudos to their teachers!

As a fifth grader I often found myself wondering whether red blood actually flowed through my teacher's veins. Despite the fact that she had the warmth of a northern Minnesota winter, I've learned over the years that the vast majority of teachers really are human beings! Unlike Mrs. Igloo (name changed to protect the guilty), they can't help but respond with more smiles, encouragement, time, and other positives to those students who help them feel good about themselves and the job they are doing. This results in a "positive interaction cycle" that spins whenever the child is around the teacher.

POLITE KIDS GET MORE KUDOS

A Positive Interaction Cycle

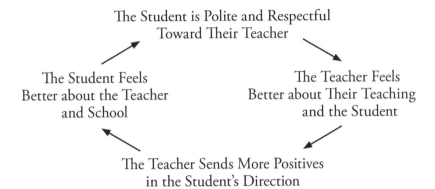

The Student is Polite and Respectful
Toward Their Teacher

The Student Feels
Better about the Teacher
and School

The Teacher Feels
Better about Their Teaching
and the Student

The Teacher Sends More Positives
in the Student's Direction

The more polite and respectful the child is, the better their teacher feels. The better their teacher feels the more positives they send in the child's direction. The more positives the child receives the better they feel about the teacher, school, and learning. The better they feel about the teacher the more they act in ways that bring the best out of their teachers. It's easy to see why these sorts of kids develop a lifelong love of learning.

Because educators are humans, too,
they can't help but respond
with more smiles, encouragement, time,
and other positives
to those students who help them
feel good about themselves.

Polite and respectful kids also have the primary attribute required for learning and achievement: an open mind. In the process of learning politeness and respect, we also learn humility. In fact, humility...or believing that we don't know everything there is to know...is critical for learning. Many of today's children have been conditioned to believe that they are smarter than their teachers. Since they've never learned sincere and humble respect for adults, they can't imagine how they might learn from them. On the other hand, kids who've been trained in politeness are far more likely to believe that teachers have plenty of knowledge and wisdom to offer.

Since politeness and respect are so important, wise adults spend at least as much time teaching them as they spend teaching academic subjects, such as math, science, history, and literature.

> *Kids who've been trained in politeness*
> *are far more likely to believe that teachers*
> *have knowledge and wisdom to offer.*

So what are some good old-fashioned strategies for giving our kids these advantages?

Model politeness, humility, thankfulness, and respect.

What do our kids overhear us saying about our jobs? Do they hear us talking about how fortunate we are to have them? Or do they mostly hear us venting about the negatives? Since thankfulness is a key ingredient of polite and respectful behavior, kids who hear their parents expressing it are far more likely to have it themselves. While it's always a challenge to watch what we say within earshot of our kids, the benefits for everyone make it worth the work.

Love and Logic Experiment

At least once a day let your kids overhear you talking about the following:

- How thankful you are to have a job.
- How smart you think your boss is.
- How smart you think their teachers are.
- How good you think their school is.
- How lucky they are to have a school.
- How much you still have to learn.
- Something exciting you've learned.
- Etc.

Remember that children tend to learn the most from the things they overhear...not the things that we try to drill into their heads with lectures.

What do your kids *experience* you saying about their school and their teachers? I use the word "experience" because the messages we send aren't always through words. Many parents say very nice things about their children's schools while at the very same time sending "your-teacher-doesn't-measure-up" messages. They do this by:

- Constantly requesting that the school or teacher change some policy or procedure they believe is either silly or unfair.
- Excusing their child from having to follow such policies or procedures.

- Constantly "educating" their child's teachers about "more effective" ways of responding to their child.
- Solving all of their child's conflicts with the teacher instead of giving their child the skills to solve them on their own.

Although most parents who do these things truly believe they are being helpful, they model the belief that schools and teachers are something one must "put up with" rather than be extremely thankful for. Kids who believe that they have to "put up with" their teachers are rarely the most respectful and responsible youngsters on the block. Even sadder, they typically transfer this attitude onto other authority figures such as employers and police officers!

Kids who believe that they have to "put up with" their teachers are rarely the most respectful and responsible youngsters on the block.

Love and Logic Experiment

Send plenty of "your-teachers-are-great" messages by:

- Expecting your child to abide by school rules and policies even when they seem a bit silly or unfair.
- Allowing your child to experience reasonable logical consequences for bad behavior or poor performance at school.
- Educate your child about how to be the most polite and respectful student in class.
- Allow your child to solve conflicts with their teachers before jumping in and doing it for them.

Remember that your child will never have a better attitude about her teachers than you do.

Give kids opportunities to be around really respectful, thankful adults.

As a child, some of the healthiest lessons I received were from the fine adults my parents chose to be their friends...or from my coaches. Because all kids experience times when they view their parents as Neanderthal-like, they also need relationships with other healthy adults in their lives to fill in these gaps. One of our most important jobs as parents is to help our kids find these healthy models.

Provide healthy alternatives to television.

Garbage in...garbage out. Much of television and the internet have become a landfill of disrespectful, impolite, and downright ill behavior. Few of us would allow our kids to spend hours each day at the local garbage dump, playing with broken bottles, dirty diapers, rotting food, and used syringes. Unfortunately, too many of us allow our kids to spend far too much time mired in electronic sewers.

(Okay, maybe I am a little bit too uptight about this issue. You can be the judge of that!)

Regardless of how tightly wound I am about this issue, I hope we can all agree that parents are wise to take an active role in making sure that their kids don't go off the cyber-screen/boob-tube deep-end. This "active role" involves helping our kids learn to take advantage of the positive aspects of this media while at the same time making healthy choices to avoid the negative.

The Love and Logic approach teaches a two-phase strategy. The first phase involves handing responsibility for setting limits over to the child. Yes! Since our children will eventually grow up and leave our protective care, it's best for them to learn how to set self-limits as soon as possible. If we start early enough, the odds go up that our kids will be really good at this critical skill by the time they encounter the most dangerous sorts of temptations.

Love and Logic Experiment

Experiment with saying the following to your child:

Do you think that I need to tell you how much TV you can watch, or do you think you can make good decisions about this for yourself? Your dad and I think that you are capable of making some really good decisions about this.

Wise parents step back and allow their kids to make these sorts of decisions, remembering that they can always take a stronger and more directive stance if their kids blow it.

Many parents are pleasantly surprised by the fact that their offspring really are capable of making good decisions. One mother commented:

It's really strange. When I tell him that he has to follow a certain rule, he almost always has to test me to see if I'm really going to stick to my guns. When I allow him to develop his own rules, he actually follows them...at least most of the time. Maybe it's because he knows that if he can't follow his rules we'll make some that are a whole lot stricter.

As implied above, sometimes kids blow it and fail to make good rules. Other times, they make good rules but they fail to live by them. Every time this happens, we can rest assured that our kids are better prepared for life...that is as long as we hold them accountable with great love and firmness.

Love and Logic Experiment

If your child is unable or unwilling to use self-control, lock in a strong dose of empathy and say:

This is so sad. Your mom and I noticed that you haven't been setting very good limits for yourself about how much time you are spending watching TV and on the internet. That's okay. Some kids just need more time before they are ready to get this sort of responsibility. We've decided that thirty minutes is the limit per day. We've also decided that we need to be with you when you are watching. When we see that you aren't arguing with us about these sorts of things, we'll know that it's time to let you start setting some of your own limits again.

Remember! Your child will be more likely to learn from this experience if you can express sadness instead of anger.

NOTHING WORKS WITHOUT THE EMPATHY.

The goal here is to send positive expectations about our kids' thinking skills while at the very same time giving them only the amount of freedom they can truly handle.

*Parents are wise to take an active role
in making sure that their kids don't go off the
cyber-screen/boob-tube deep-end.*

Expect politeness and thankfulness.

Are your kids in the habit of saying "please" and "thank you"? If not, there's no time to waste! Although my parents weren't perfect, they did help us understand that polite and thankful behavior was the only way we'd get the things that we really wanted from them. The moment we acted the least bit demanding or entitled was the moment they stopped providing any sort of privilege or perk.

All kids experiment with being a bit nasty from time to time. It's our job as parents to prove to them that they will get more with honey than vinegar. Unfortunately, I see too many children who get their way by demanding, arguing, and throwing fits. It doesn't take a rocket scientist to figure out why these kids have such a hard time in school. Since they believe that manipulation is the best way to get what they want, they feel it extremely unfair when their teachers expect them to earn their grades through good old-fashioned hard work.

Love and Logic Experiment

Memorize the following statement, and use it whenever your kids become demanding or ungrateful:

I do things for people who say "please" and "thank you."

As you repeat this, be certain to model a polite and respect-ful attitude. Wise parents remember that getting snippy and sarcastic with their kids ruins the learning opportunity.

Obviously your children will not be overjoyed that you've decided to do these sorts of things! When we are willing to allow our children to get really upset in the short-term, the odds go up that they will learn a variety of skills that contribute to academic success…and a great life:

- Delayed gratification
- Patience
- Self-control
- Respect for authority figures

> *All kids experiment with being a bit nasty*
> *from time to time. It's our job as parents to*
> *prove to them that they will get more*
> *with honey than vinegar.*

Reward politeness and thankfulness.

Rewards are like any other technique: Their long-term effectiveness depends entirely on how they are used. Listed below is a comparison between the effective and less-than-effective use of rewards:

Effective: The child understands that they won't always receive tangible rewards for polite and respectful behavior.

Ineffective: The child comes to expect tangible rewards for acting polite.

Effective: The child never knows for sure when a reward will come.

Ineffective: The child can always predict when they will receive a reward, so they act nice only at these times.

Effective: The adult provides occasional rewards when it's fun for the adult.

Ineffective: The adult provides rewards (actually bribes) because they feel it's the only way to make the child behave.

Effective: The adult provides rewards only when the child does not expect them.

Ineffective: The adult provides rewards even when the child demands them.

What's the bottom line? Successful adults provide "surprise rewards."

Love and Logic Experiment

When all is going well, and you are excited about your child's sweet behavior, say:

I really appreciate how polite and helpful you have been. It's really fun for me to do _____ when kids act that way. Thanks!

Go do something fun together. Enjoy!

Politeness as an Insurance Policy

All summed up, making a big deal out of teaching politeness and respect essentially provides youngsters with an insurance policy. Kids given this gift are far more likely to overcome tough life circumstances. Consider the following:

- If…as an adult…your polite and respectful child finds herself competing with another employee for a promotion, might her sweet disposition give her at least a small edge?
- If…as an adult…your polite and respectful child finds himself working for a company engaging in massive layoffs, might his great character make it a little less likely that he'll lose his job?
- If your polite and respectful child experiences a layoff anyway, will he have better letters of recommendation…and more new job prospects…than his less positive peers?
- If your polite and respectful child experiences serious learning problems, and never gets high grades, might her great character allow her to experience a great life, anyway?

In my lifetime, I've met countless people who've made a career out of being polite and respectful. Many of them never earned good grades as kids. Many of them never had an opportunity to attend college. All of them experienced seemingly insurmountable economic and family circumstances. They overcame these obstacles for one simple reason:

> *They were extremely pleasant to be around,*
> *leaving those who crossed their paths*
> *feeling great about themselves.*

If we can teach our children how to achieve this simple goal, will they be lifetime high achievers…regardless of how well they do on the big tests? If we can give them the gift of graciousness, will they succeed regardless of how good or bad their report cards look when they are children?

Will you please give this some careful thought? Thank you!

Chores at Home are Critical for School and Life Success

So…why are we all so obsessed with homework?

Which is going to help our kids the most in life? Will it be the homework they lug home in their backpacks…or the chores they complete as loved and needed members of the family? In today's academically anxious world, many seem confused…even annoyed… by this question. "Homework!" they howl. "Chores are important," they concede, "but not nearly as important as homework!"

Is it possible that we as a society have placed the cart before the horse? Is it even possible that many of us have forgotten all about the horse?

What do horses, carts, and their relative positions have to do with academic success?

Both are important. If we want our children to have the skills required for successful competition in tomorrow's competitive job market, they'll need to arrive at that market with a cart heavily laden with knowledge. Of course, to get there in the first place, they'll need a strong and dependable horse, willing to pull that cart over many steep hills.

The cart represents all of the academic skills they will learn from schoolwork and homework.

The horse represents the character required to stay motivated and focused in a world full of temptations.

These days lots of carts are getting to market without their horses. How does such a strange thing happen? As far as I can figure, plenty of carts must be getting pulled by well-meaning parents and educators who want so badly for kids to achieve that they are willing to achieve for them. The owners of these carts show up for work with good transcripts. Many even show up with plenty of knowledge. The problem is that many of them haven't a clue how to unload their carts and actually apply this knowledge when the going gets tough…or when work actually feels like…work.

Based on decades of experience, we at the Love and Logic Institute have observed that children who complete real and meaningful chores…without reminders and without pay…are far better students than those who don't. Why is this so? Discussed below are just a few of the reasons:

Chores teach self-control, perseverance, and delayed gratification.

When children are expected to make contributions to the family requiring sustained effort and sacrifice, they learn how to display these same qualities at school. They also get the practice they need to eventually display these character attributes at work and in their marriages.

Is it possible that a large number of the problems we face as a nation have to do with the belief among many that a lifetime of happiness and self-fulfillment shouldn't require more time or effort than heating a frozen burrito in the microwave? Not long ago almost everything was more difficult and time-consuming.

- Do you remember when we had to wait to make a phone call until we either got home or found a pay phone?
- Do you remember when we had to take the time to send real letters in the mail…instead of emailing or texting?
- Do you remember when we had to leave home to buy the things we needed…instead of shopping online?
- Do you remember when we had to use those slow things called typewriters?
- Do you remember a time when most people had to actually pay in full before having in full?
- Is it possible that some of us even remember when it was more difficult and time-consuming to get divorced than it was to get married?

> *A large number of our nation's problems*
> *have to do with the belief among many*
> *that a lifetime of happiness*
> *and self-fulfillment*
> *shouldn't require more time or effort*
> *than heating a frozen burrito*
> *in the microwave.*

Could it be that our microwave world has led many youngsters to believe that their teachers are crazy for expecting them to sacrifice the time and effort required for learning?

Love and Logic Experiment

Teach your kids to cook. Teach them to do it the old-fashioned way without a microwave. Of course, for some of us this requires that we teach ourselves as we teach our kids! The skills learned from planning, preparing, and cleaning up after a family meal will serve your children well in many areas of their lives. These skills include organization, multitasking, self-control, delayed gratification, etc. An added benefit is this:

They get to feel like important and appreciated members of the family!

Chores meet the need for structure and limits.

When children lack structure and limits one of the first things seen is a decline in academic motivation and performance. Because the safety provided by firm and loving limits is such a critical need, the brain filters out everything else in a single-minded obsession with getting it met.

How can we know when we've let this portion of our parental duties slip? Do our kids come to us and say:

Mom…Dad…we're all feeling really uneasy about the fact that you aren't setting firm limits with us. It makes us wonder if we are safe. In fact, our subconscious minds are spending so much time worrying about this issue that we aren't able to focus on school. We would really like you guys to take your parenting up a notch and show us that you love us enough to set some limits.

Yeah right! This will probably happen about the same time that the sun begins to orbit the earth.

People…not just kids…communicate their need for firmer limits by acting out, being demanding, acting angrily, and/or developing a severe case of entitlement. When we fall into the trap of appeasement, their sense of hostile dependency deepens…and they become progressively more out-of-control.

Chores are a gift! Chores provide an opportunity for our beloved children to experience limits.

For these limits to be effective, they must be over matters within our control. They must be enforceable. They must give us an opportunity to prove that what comes out of our mouths will always happen.

Most of us have learned a bitter truth: We can't control the actions of others. Unfortunately, too many of us fall into the trap of issuing threats instead of real limits.

> *Limits involve what we know we can do.*
> *Threats involve what we wish we could do.*

The Love and Logic approach teaches one basic rule about setting effective limits:

> *Never tell a stubborn child what to do.*
> *Describe what you are willing to do or allow instead.*

When we follow this important rule, we set enforceable limits using enforceable statements. When we follow this critical guideline, we focus on the controllable…rather than the uncontrollable. Listed below are some examples:

Enforceable Statement	**Less Effective Statement**
(Focusing on the controllable)	*(Focusing on the uncontrollable)*
I provide dinner when the chores are done.	Take out the trash. Do it now!
I will take you to your friend's house when your chores are done.	There is no way that I am driving you anywhere until you do your chores.
I'll be happy to do the extra things I do for you when I don't have to remind you to finish your chores.	I am sick and tired of having to remind you. You need to do things the first time I ask.
I charge $25 per hour to do other people's chores. Are you planning to pay me or do them yourself?	Why are you watching TV? Aren't you supposed to be cleaning the bathroom? Last week you never did it and I had to take a bunch of time out of my own schedule to get it done.
You may keep the things that you pick up.	I keep the things that I pick up.

Love and Logic Experiment

For a week or two, experiment with using just one of the enforceable statements listed above. Say it sweetly and say it once. Remind yourself not to remind your child…then let the consequence do the teaching. Prepare yourself for an upset and argumentative kid.

If you hear something like, "Not fair!" or "Why do you treat me like a slave?" repeat with love in your voice, "I love you too much to argue."

Regardless of the argument, softly repeat, "I love you too much to argue."

NOTHING WORKS WITHOUT THE EMPATHY.

Chores meet the need to be needed.

When kids feel unneeded, they feel lost. When they feel lost, they're far less likely to complete schoolwork and homework. Again, their subconscious minds are focused on meeting needs far more basic than academic achievement.

This need to belong and feel important is so critical that many youth eventually join gangs in a desperate attempt to get it met. Dramatically reduce the odds of this by establishing your own "gang" at home. A key element of gang membership is that every person in the family (i.e. "gang member") has critical responsibilities that contribute to the welfare of the entire gang…and each gang member is held accountable for their performance of these duties. Beginning no later than age four, children should be acting as important members of the family gang, doing their fair share to make the entire operation run as smoothly as possible.

Love and Logic Experiment

Sit down by yourself and make a list of all of the things required to keep your house and family running smoothly. Then ask yourself, "Which of these are my children capable of doing?" If your kids can do something, they probably should be. Remember that everything we do for them is something they may never learn to do for themselves.

Beginning no later than age four,
children should be acting as important members
of the family gang, doing their fair share
to make the entire operation run as
smoothly as possible.

Early in our country's history, children were depended upon in very real and tangible ways as contributors to the family economy. I'm very thankful that we've moved beyond treating many children as sweatshop slaves. I'm not so thankful that the pendulum has swung to the other extreme! Far too many of us expect far too little from our children.

Perhaps children growing up in loving farm families had the best of both worlds. They experienced serious responsibilities at home involving plenty of chores. They also enjoyed opportunities to take breaks and go to school. Many who grew up this way comment, "I always looked forward to going to school because I got to play with my friends and do easier things like schoolwork."

Chores make schoolwork and homework seem easy.

If we expect very little from our children at home, should we be surprised when they complain about school being too hard? When we fail to expect enough help from them at home, we create a fantasy world in their heads. When their school or life experience fails to match this utopian vision, they become disgruntled, disobedient, and unmotivated in their studies. The ultimate irony is that parents who expect their children to work hard on chores create children who are typically far happier as they encounter the realities of life. It's as if their children reason, "Hey! School and life are kind of a piece of cake compared to all of the jobs I've got to do at home." Of course, this only happens within the context of a loving family where children are also allowed to do what children need to do: Play! Have you noticed that success in just about everything involves balance?

Chores build self-esteem.

Although I never enjoyed starting my chores, I always enjoyed looking back and seeing that I'd finished them! Part of this involved the relief of getting them over with, whereas a larger part represented feelings of pride in a job well done. Over the last fifty years, educators and mental health professionals have searched...largely in vain...for some magic bullet that would enable all children to feel great about themselves. While their quest has been a noble one, many seem to have spun their wheels in the sand of "feel good" psychology. The deceptive premise of this perspective goes something like the following:

If we do whatever we can to make children feel comfortable and praised all of the time, they will feel good about themselves and will want to be high achievers.

Wouldn't it be great if it really worked that way! Here's the truth about doing everything for kids:

If we do whatever we can to make children feel comfortable and praised all of the time, they begin to feel like they can't make it in life without somebody praising them and making them feel comfortable all of the time.
     It doesn't take long before they feel completely helpless AND resentful toward the ones who make them feel that way.

All of us were wired to develop the greatest feelings of accomplishment and self-esteem while doing things that contribute to the welfare of others. That's why the true formula for building self-esteem involves expecting our children to participate as real and desperately needed members of the family team.

Tips for Getting Chores Done without Reminders and Without Pay.

While the case for chores over homework is a solid one, it doesn't mean a thing if we don't have practical and effective tools for teaching our kids to do them. Listed below are tips for making this happen.

Tip One

Firmly commit yourself to the notion that chores are more important than homework, sports, music lessons, or anything else.

Yes! We do believe that chores are more important than these activities. Believe it or not, we even believe that they ought to take precedence over video games, TV, and Twittering. Until we make the mental and emotional commitment to this notion, it's unlikely we'll stay firmly rooted when we receive pressure from friends, relatives, neighbors, coworkers, educators, advertisers, and our own youngsters to back down. Until we firmly believe in our heads and in our hearts that chores are more important than homework…or just about anything else…we won't have the intestinal fortitude to stick to our guns when our kids have snits, fits, and say things like, "The only reason you had kids it to make them into slaves. None of my friends have to do all of this crap. Their parents love them."

Like many of the most effective things we do as parents, putting this emphasis on chores probably won't win us any "Most Beloved Parent of the Year" awards. The good feelings come later as our kids grow, mature, and begin to realize that maybe we do have more than barnyard waste between our ears. If we're mentally and emotionally prepared for a bit of rebellion in the short-term, we're far more likely to experience plenty of respect and responsibility out of our kids in the long-term.

Love and Logic Experiment

When your kids complain and say, "Kim's parents don't make her do chores," reply with a sweet smile, "That's so sad for Kim."

Each time they complain about this, simply repeat your response in a lovingly sad tone, "I know. That is so sad for Kim."

It won't take long before your kids realize that using this manipulative ploy won't excuse them from their domestic duties.

Tip Two

Firmly commit yourself to the notion that chores must be completed without warnings and reminders.

Kids will always come to need at least the same number of warnings and reminders as we give them. That's why it's helpful…if we'd like them to experience a lifetime of scholastic and occupational disappointments…

to give them at least three or four before we follow through with consequences. Yep! Children who are nagged and reminded to do their chores typically expect the same treatment out of their teachers and their future employers.

A powerful trick for resisting the urge to nag or remind is to flip your mindset around to looking forward to mistakes. That's right! Love and Logic parents look forward to their children making affordable mistakes. That's because they understand that the "price tag" of mistakes increases every day.

When do you want your kids to refuse or forget to complete their responsibilities? Would it be best for this to happen when they are young and the consequences are relatively small? Or would it be best for them to make these blunders when they're older and the consequences are far greater…possibly life and death?

Kids learn to make great decisions about big and important things by making plenty of poor decisions about relatively small, unimportant things…and experiencing the natural, logical consequences. When we make the paradigm switch to viewing mistakes as affordable learning opportunities, it becomes much easier to keep our mouths shut instead of nagging and reminding.

Love and Logic Experiment

If you've already fallen into the habit of giving too many warnings or reminders, say to your child:

I'm so sorry. I've been treating you like a little kid who needs to be nagged all of the time to do their chores. Would you like it better if I got off your back? From now on, I'm going to do my best to treat you like an adult.

What your child won't know until later is that "being treated like an adult" also means that you won't be shielding them from the consequences of failing to do their chores.

Tip Three

Firmly commit yourself to the notion that chores must be completed without pay.

In today's me-centered world, are there already enough people who won't lift a finger without getting something in return? Sadly, what these folks don't seem to understand is that getting paid for everything short-circuits the rewarding feelings achieved when we contribute out of the goodness of our hearts.

Do you want your kids to grow up believing that the road to fulfillment involves having the biggest bank account? Or…would you be prouder if they matured to understand that true happiness comes from helping and sharing?

Love and Logic Experiment

If you'd like to stop paying your kids to do their chores, say to them,

We realize that we've been stealing from you. We've been robbing you of the good feelings and good character that come from helping without being paid to do it.

We also recommend making a nice little refrigerator sign reading,

We help each other because we love each other.

Every time your kids complain about not being paid for chores, repeat in a loving tone of voice, "We help each other because we love each other."

Tip Four

Teach your kids exactly what you expect.

Wise parents spend some time describing…and even practicing… the chores they want their children to do. Spending a Saturday afternoon training and practicing can go a long way toward helping your children feel more competent and less resistant about helping out.

Love and Logic Experiment

Some youngsters...particularly younger ones or ones with special needs...need more reminders. To give them coping skills for life, however, these reminders need to come from themselves.

One of the most enjoyable strategies for accomplishing this involves taking pictures of your child completing each of their different chores. Stick these up on their bedroom wall along with pictures of a clock representing when they need to be completed.

Other kids simply need to keep a good list, learn to use a schedule book, or enter their responsibilities into one of those nifty newfangled electronic calendar devices.

An added benefit of doing this is that the list...or the pictures...or the schedule book can be the "bad guy." Instead of always being the bearer of bad news, you can simply empathize by saying,

Sometimes I feel the very same way. Sometimes I don't want to do what's on my list either. I love you. Hang in there.

When we teach our kids exactly what we expect, we cut down on resistance and give organizational skills that will serve them for a lifetime.

Tip Five

When giving a chore, don't say, "Do it now!" Give them a deadline, instead.

Smart parents say, "Just have this done by your bedtime," or "Just have this done by Sunday at 6 p.m."

What sort of employer would you rather work for? One who consistently demanded immediate compliance...or one who respected you enough to give reasonable deadlines?

There's an added benefit of this approach, as well: It gives us plenty of time to figure out what we'll do if our kids either become resistant or memory-impaired!

Tip Six

Remind yourself to avoid giving reminders.

At the risk of being ironic, I'd like to remind you that the road to wisdom is paved with mistakes and their consequences. I'd also like to remind you that reminding our kids so that they don't make mistakes has four very unfortunate results:

1. We rob them of affordable learning opportunities.
2. We get them "addicted" to reminders.
3. We severely damage our relationship with them.
4. We become so tired and worn out that we no longer enjoy our kids.

Tip Seven

Resist the urge to become a cheerleader.

Too frequently parents and educators have been told to gush massive amounts of praise and adulation whenever kids do something good. Although we're big fans of being positive and encouraging with children, we know that cheerleader behavior typically gets kids addicted to needing cheerleading.

Since it's unlikely that our kids will have the personal income needed to hire 24 hour a day personal pompom shakers, they're better off if we simply notice what they've done, pat them on the back, smile and say:

Thanks. I bet it feels great to have that done!

Notice that this statement keeps most of the good feelings on the kid...rather than the adult. I think most of us can agree that we want our kids to be motivated from the inside-out rather than the outside-in.

Love and Logic Experiment

Notice and describe instead of using praise. In other words, when your child does something well, say,

I noticed that you _____.

Resist the urge to add something like, "That's great!" on the end of this. While I guarantee that it'll probably feel pretty weird to you and your child, I also guarantee that it will have far better results than piling on the praise.

Tip Eight

Let consequences wrapped in empathy do the teaching.

When our kids fail to complete their chores...or the job they do is clearly substandard...we have a number of possible options:

- Do the chore for them and have them pay us for the time we spent. They can "pay" us by doing some of our most unattractive chores, staying home instead of being taken somewhere they want to go, giving us one of their favorite toys, etc.
- Say, "I'll be happy to do the extra things I do for you when I don't have to spend my time doing your chores." Then go on strike and negotiate for better working conditions.
- Say, "I allow use of the car when I don't have to worry about you forgetting to do your chores."
- Hire a professional to complete the job to allow your child to pay for the cost with one of their favorite possessions. Along these lines, we know one mother who provided her daughter with the wonderful learning experience of paying a maid service to clean her room!
- Any other reasonably logical consequence that helps your child realize that their lives are a lot more fun and rewarding when they remember to do their chores.

Generally speaking, the consequence we use is far less important than how we deliver it. Providing genuine sadness and empathy... rather than sarcasm or anger...is essential!

NOTHING WORKS WITHOUT THE EMPATHY.

Love and Logic Experiment

One way to make your use of empathy more automatic is to memorize just one empathetic phrase. Use this same one each and every time you need to provide a consequence.

Examples include:

This is so sad…	What a bummer…	How sad…
This stinks…	That's never good…	Dang…

Successful parents write their favorite phrase on sticky notes and post it all over the house. Repeated exposure to this phrase dramatically ups the odds you'll remember to be sad and empathetic… instead of frustrated, angry, or sarcastic.

Help them when they're working hard.

When you see your children working their tails off completing chores, ask them if you can help. Help as long as they are working hard, and comment on how good it makes you feel to help out and to spend time with them. When you're old and gray, wouldn't it be great if they'd come over and do the same for you? The odds are dramatically increased when we make this investment.

Years ago a woman at one of my conferences shared a powerful testimony to the critical importance of chores for children:

Our father was mostly out of the picture when we were kids, so mom had to work her fingers to the bone making sure that we had everything that we needed and wanted. She did such a good job that we all became a little spoiled and bratty. Then she was diagnosed with cancer, and this changed everything. She was so sick from the chemotherapy that most of the time she couldn't even get the basics done for us. When this happened, we were forced to do our fair share just to keep the family going.

"That must have been really tough!" I commented.

Yes, it was! But it also forced us to learn a lot and to contribute to the family for its survival. When mom passed away, we all went to live with our grandparents. They gave us plenty of love and plenty of chores. When things settled down enough for us to focus on school, we all seemed to appreciate it more than ever before. It was horrible that mom suffered so much and ended up passing on, but being forced to help our family survive really made us stronger and more responsible in the long run.

While we'd never wish this tragic situation on anyone, it does illustrate the profound power of chores in shaping responsibility, self-esteem, and gratitude. Children with these core character attributes are the same children who excel in school and in life.

The question for all of us is:

Are we doing our part to help *our* kids enjoy this advantage?

Does Your Child Have Too Much Stuff?

Kids are more likely to work when they have something to work toward.

Why are there so many kids who won't lift a finger to do their schoolwork?" This question...asked by educators everywhere I travel... has many answers. In the introduction to this book I discussed the well-established scientific fact that the human brain filters out information that is not directly relevant to meeting basic physical and emotional needs. The direct result is that children appear academically disinterested, resistant, or downright lazy when they are distracted by these unmet needs. In previous chapters I've also advanced the unorthodox idea that the solutions to academic apathy have more to do with meeting these needs than implementing the correct testing procedures, rewards, consequences, or government programs.

In a nutshell, successful educators and parents understand that long-term solutions require a consistent focus on two things:

• Rebuilding the foundation of basic needs...so that children are capable of focusing on learning.

• Teaching children how to display good character...so that they have what it really takes to be successful in life.

In previous chapters I've also emphasized the importance of:

• Helping children identify and build upon their natural gifts...so they have the self-esteem required to tackle their weaknesses.
• Teaching them to display politeness and respect...so that others feel good about them and they can feel good about themselves.
• Expecting them to complete chores without reminders and without pay...so that their need to be needed is fulfilled.

Distilled to its simplest form, solving the problem of chronic underachievement involves asking the following question:

How can we up the odds that children
will no longer be distracted
by unmet needs or by their own
poor behavior?

Answering this question involves taking a fresh look at why so many kids are so chronically distracted.

The More Obvious Examples

Sometimes the answer is obvious, as in cases where children live in constant need. Because of the poverty they experience on a daily basis, their minds focus on hunger pangs, worries about where they will live tomorrow, whether they'll be safe on the way home from school, etc.

Many children appear lazy at school because they are distracted by the fact that they have to be parents to their parents. Anyone who's worked in the schools for more than a day or two has met these children. An example from my past is permanently seared into my memory. He always remains in my thoughts because of the dire nature of his home life…as well as how poorly we responded to him at school.

He spent most of his time in class sleeping. Insulted by his lack of academic drive, we at the school resorted to all sorts of punishments designed to light a fire under his apathetic britches. It wasn't until halfway through the year that we learned the truth about him: He slept through every class because he spent every night waiting in the car outside of tawdry bars. He dozed every day because every night he waited in that car for his mother to stagger out of the door. He lacked academic motivation because at 2 a.m. every morning, after the last call for alcohol, he'd drive his mother home from these bars. He was twelve years old.

The true solution to this boy's underachievement involved reporting the situation to Child Protective Services, getting him placed with people who would nurture him, and showing him massive levels of understanding and unconditional love at school. To this day I still experience appropriate pangs of guilt remembering how long we punished this child before we discovered what he really needed to succeed.

The Less Obvious Examples

A wise psychologist friend of mine often remarked:

The effect of the opposite is often the same.

What she meant by this is that opposite parenting styles or family situations often create kids with similar problems. Parents who are harsh often create angry kids. So do parents who fail to set limits and try to be their child's best friend. Parents who are overinvolved in trying to "fix" all of their children's problems often create kids who feel weak and incapable. So do parents who couldn't care less about their children's problems. Kids who've been neglected often feel like the world owes them everything. Kids who've been overindulged often have the very same perspective.

As we saw above, kids who are distracted by having too little display very little interest in school. These are the obvious cases, where we say to each other, "Of course that child isn't motivated to learn!"

The less obvious cases represent those children who have way too much. These are the children that leave us scratching our heads, wondering, "She has everything she wants. Why is she so disinterested in school?"

What's the answer? Because she has everything she wants…and it gets in the way of her getting what she needs.

In today's America, we have an epidemic of youngsters who live in a constant state of distraction brought on by exposure to a constant cornucopia of fun stuff and fun activities. Even in today's tough economy, we see more and more children developing ADD…a different type of ADD:

Affluence Distraction Disorder

Is it any surprise that so many children lack motivation in school when so many believe that they've already "arrived"? Prior to the 1950s most American children grew up without many of the things they wanted. Because of this, most imagined what it might be like to someday struggle above their meager circumstances and "arrive" at a more comfortable standard of living. Getting a good education was seen as the primary vehicle for attaining this dream. Over the last five decades, the amount of unneeded stuff possessed by many American children has dramatically squelched this dreaming process. There's no need to dream or work toward things you already have.

> ### *There's no need to dream or work toward things you already have.*

The problem has reached epic proportions! In fact, many kids have so many goodies that they experience little or no concern when something gets broken, lost, or taken away as a consequence for bad behavior. One woman commented:

> *We started this new plan in our home where we would allow our six-year-old to keep only those toys she picked up without having to be nagged or reminded. It took almost two weeks before she even flinched as a result of our keeping the toys she left out. In fact, one day she calmly informed me, "Mom, you can pick those up. I don't want them." Now that she has a small number of treasured possessions, things have really changed. Now, she screams anytime it looks like I'm going to pick them up, "Mom! I want those!" Then she runs over and puts them away.*

A few days ago I visited my great aunt. She was born in 1909... so she's seen a few changes in her lifetime! Still sharp, she recalled being rather "spoiled" as a child since she had two dolls instead of just one.

In today's America, how many children would feel fortunate to have only two handmade toys? Have many of us lost touch with what our children really need? Is it possible that we've focused so much on what they want...that we're failing to provide what they need?

> *Even in today's tough economy,*
> *there's an epidemic of children with a different type*
> *of ADD: Affluence Distraction Disorder.*

How do sensible parents fall into the trap of raising kids with Affluence Distraction Disorder? Listed below are some of the most common mistakes, as well as solutions.

Mistake #1

Believing that lecturing kids about life's struggles is a substitute for allowing them to experience some of them.

I often wonder if all humans are born with a certain portion of the brain that remains dormant until they become parents. This "lecture lobe" contains all of the lectures given by all of our ancestors, as well as the capacity to create new ones at a moment's notice. Right next to the one about certain toys putting your eye out, the one about starving kids in China, and the one urging the importance of wearing clean underwear (just in case you get in an accident and the paramedics have to remove your pants) is the one about life not being fair and how you might just have to dig ditches if you don't do your schoolwork and homework.

I'm not quite sure when these lectures actually worked. What I am sure of is how utterly ineffective they are with today's children. I have yet to meet a youth who suddenly became enthused about avoiding BB guns, eating spinach, wearing clean shorts, or getting a good education as a result of hearing a lecture.

Some folks continue to hold out hope. It's as if they reason, "I just haven't used this lecture enough. At some point, perhaps after my child has heard it 23,000 times, he will suddenly jump out of his chair and scream, 'I see the light!'"

Is time with our kids too precious to waste on ineffective techniques?

Solution #1

Replace lectures with plenty of opportunities for your children to struggle toward earning some of the things they want.

There's nothing that teaches kids about the real world better than simulating it for them as they are growing up. If we want our kids to grasp the immense importance of education and of handling money wisely, they'll need to experience what it feels like to want...and what if feels like to do without...and what it feels like to have some things that they've worked hard to have. The earlier and more consistently they experience these feelings, the happier and more successful they'll be!

Love and Logic Experiment

Write the following phrase on a bunch of sticky notes:

You may have _____ when you can pay for it.

Post these notes in places where you'll see them often: on your alarm clock, the refrigerator, the dashboard of your car, inside your purse or wallet, etc. Seeing it often will up the odds that you'll say it often.

While I'm not against being generous and buying our kids some of the things they want, I've noticed that the most successful adults grew up having to earn most of the extra things they wanted as kids.

Another option involves helping our children by paying a certain amount of the total. When our child asks for a $150 dollar pair of jeans, we might reply, "Those look great! I'll pay $20 toward them. If you can come up with the remainder, they're yours."

Mistake #2

Believing that giving your kids lots of stuff will make them want to earn a similar lifestyle when they are grown.

"My husband and I believe that our children will be more likely to want a good education if we allow them to have plenty of luxuries. When they acquire a taste for the finer things in life, they will want to work hard so that they'll be able to have them as adults."

If I didn't hear this distorted logic so often, I wouldn't be wasting ink and paper bringing it up in this book. Yep! Some parents truly believe that spoiling their kids will result in them having a strong drive to acquire good grades and a good education.

Solution #2

Remind yourself that giving your kids too much leads to a sense of entitlement.

While it would be nice if kids appreciated everything we gave them, the truth is that most feel more deprived each and every time we shower them with more stuff. Instead of feeling appreciative, they become like drug addicts, desperate for another fix. Instead of being thankful for what they have, they become angry, sullen, and dependent upon the excitement of always being given something new and exciting.

Kids who are addicted to drugs never do well in school. Kids who are addicted to stuff don't either. Because they believe that they are entitled to all of the perks of success...without having to earn them...they feel insulted when their teachers suggest that they work hard and earn their grades.

An entitled child's belief about school:
Since everything in life is free,
my grades should be, too!

Love and Logic Experiment

If you've fallen into this trap of giving your kids too much, it's never too late to apologize to them:

We are so sorry. We've been stealing from you. By giving you so many things, we've robbed you of opportunities to feel really proud of yourself by earning things.

Don't expect your kids to say something like, "What a relief! It's about time you figured out that I'll be happier and more responsible if I see a connection between what I have and how hard I've worked for it. Thanks so much!"

Do be ready to say:

You may have _____ when you can pay for it.

In the previous chapter I discussed the importance of empathy. Will you be more successful saying, "You may have _ when you can pay for it," if your voice is filled with compassion instead of sarcasm? Will your child be more likely to eventually view you as loving and wise if you can say this with sadness instead of anger? Will your son or daughter be less likely to become resentful and rebellious if you can demonstrate that you really care about their desires even if you aren't planning to fulfill them?

NOTHING WORKS WITHOUT THE EMPATHY.

Mistake #3

Forgetting that your kids see your lifestyle as it is now... not what it was before you earned it.

Many children, particularly those of older parents, aren't aware of how hard their parents had to work to earn the lifestyle they are currently enjoying. Even when these parents are careful to avoid giving too much, it's easy for their kids to start believing that comfortable houses, shiny cars, and other great stuff magically appears when a person gets older. To make matters more difficult, many older parents have struggled so hard in life that they want to start enjoying the fruits of their labor...by having some nicer things. While there's certainly nothing wrong with this, it is a bit more challenging to raise appreciative, highly motivated kids.

Solution #3

Help your children learn how you've earned what you have.

This solution has two parts: The first involves giving your kids a glimpse of what your lifestyle was like in the past. The second involves showing them how to delay gratification today.

Love and Logic Experiment

Give your kids a glimpse at how hard you've had to struggle:

- At least once a week allow them to overhear you reminiscing about how hard you had to struggle to earn what you now have.
- As often as possible, share stories with them about the economic struggles you've encountered. Do this without taking on a lecturing tone.
- Show them pictures of where you lived, the car you drove, etc.
- Encourage their grandparents to do the same.

Have you noticed that youngsters seem to listen a lot more carefully when they overhear us talking...than when we try to impart our wisdom through lectures? Smart parents set it up so that their kids frequently overhear them reminiscing about the junky old cars they had to drive, the difficult jobs they worked, the run-down apartments they lived in, and all of the hard work and time it took to earn what they now have. Our attitude is critical here! If they overhear us complaining about how hard life has been this won't have the desired effect. If instead they overhear us reminiscing with joy and satisfaction, the odds go up that they'll begin to get the picture that all of this good stuff didn't just magically appear.

Wise parents also share their stories directly with their kids by looking at old pictures, visiting past homes and workplaces, and talking fondly about their struggles. Typically kids are quite interested in this information when they don't feel like it's being used to set them straight.

While sharing our past can be fun and easy, showing them that we're willing to delay gratification...today...can be tough. Even in today's difficult economy, many parents have the means to buy themselves many things they don't really need. The only way our children will learn how to work hard in school and wait for what they want is by seeing our example.

Do your kids ever see you resisting the urge to buy yourself the things you want?

Love and Logic Experiment

Let your kids see you resisting the urge to buy some of the things you want. While this may be one of the most challenging parenting "skills" to exercise, it will surely pay off big time in the end.

Also let your kids overhear you thinking out loud as you resist this urge. They need to hear you thinking things like:

I really want this badly. Oh man. I better wait until I know for sure I can afford it.

And...

This looks great. I really want it.
But...I'm not sure it's going to make me as happy as I think it will.

And...

I want that, but I think it would be better for me to save for a rainy day.

Mistake #4

Failing to have a plan for handling excessive gift-giving by extended family and friends.

Even when we do our very best to avoid buying our kids too many things, many of us find that the stuff piles up anyway. Because we don't want to hurt anyone's feelings, many of us shy away from asking family and friends to tone down their generosity.

I'm really not a scrooge. Really! I'm not as mean as my reputation suggests! I think it's great for kids to get nice gifts, but I also know that things can really get out of hand.

Solution #4

Encourage family and friends to avoid buying too much, and encourage your kids to donate toys to less fortunate families.

Okay, I'll be the bad guy. Just hand this book to family and friends so they'll be upset with me instead of you. If it makes things any easier, you can share it with your kids, too.

Wise parents take a proactive approach. Before holidays, birthdays, and other special occasions, they allow their kids to overhear them talking about how fortunate their family is...and how many families are struggling. They also allow their kids to overhear them talking about how they are planning to donate at least one of the gifts they receive. When children know that their parents are willing to make these small sacrifices, they're far more likely to do the same.

Love and Logic Experiment

Show your kids that giving is more important than receiving.

- Do this by donating at least one gift item you've received to someone in need.
- Have them come along as you deliver it or drop it in a donation box.
- Strongly encourage your youngsters to do the same.
- The items donated should be new...not throwaway junk.

Time and time again I'm amazed by the therapeutic effects of extending generosity. Thus, I've become convinced that we as human beings are wired to need it. At the rate with which modern science is progressing, I also believe that before very long, brain researchers will identify specific regions of the brain that stimulate good feelings and tranquility when people engage in giving. (By the way, if you know of this research let me know!)

Mistake #5

Worrying about what other people will think.

If we do the things required to raise really responsible, ethical, and motivated kids, some people are going to think that we are very, very strange. Others may even accuse us of being selfish or downright mean. For some parents this is far too high a price to pay. Wiser ones remember that the stakes are way too high to be worrying about what other people think.

Solution #5

With love in your heart be willing to be the strangest parent on the block.

As you already know, the Love and Logic approach is not about being mean or selfish. It is all about preparing kids for the real world by simulating that world in our homes each and every day. Sure, practicing to become a successful adult is hard work! Yes, it's fraught with some struggle, disappointment, and frustration. By providing big doses of love and empathy as our kids learn to cope, we send a powerfully motivating message:

> *We love you and we know that you*
> *have what it takes to learn*
> *how to cope with this challenging world!*

Although we might look like the strangest parents on the block, we'll dramatically increase the odds that our kids will understand that nothing in life is free...and that earning an education and marketable skills is well worth the effort.

Dramatic reminders of the curse of entitlement can be found in the sad lives of so many children of the Hollywood or social elite. All it takes is one look at the gossip magazines or television "entertainment" shows to see how messed up kids get when they are given everything they want. What a train wreck these lives become! Sadly, they stand as living, breathing examples of why it's so important to let our children struggle.

As I write this section, the great granddaughter of a rather famous hotel magnate comes to mind.

The most important things you can do...

- Spend as much time as you possibly can with your kids.
- Play with them.
- Listen to them.
- Comfort them when they are hurting.
- Rejoice with them when they are glad.
- Enjoy them with all of your heart.

When children have parents who give the greatest gifts...their love and their time...they don't care as much about having lots of expensive stuff.

Would You Like a Calmer, More Motivated Child?

A dull home makes school more exciting!

If you remember your first personal computer, you probably remember how much work you got done while using it. Yep! My 80s-era machine was great. While waiting for it to perform basic functions, such as opening or saving a file, I was able to clean my apartment, make a few phone calls, take a shower, and tune up the car. Back in those days I got a lot done.

These days I never get anything accomplished! Even on this relatively archaic laptop, things happen so fast that it leaves time for nothing else. Of course, this doesn't stop me from complaining about how "slow" this machine can be. Milliseconds seem like decades as I wait for it to download massive amounts of data.

Have I become a bit spoiled?

What do my seemingly random musings over computer memory have to do with underachievement among today's youth?

Is it possible that many kids have become so addicted to the fast-paced stimulation of modern technology that they view their teachers as archaic machines in need of quicker hard drives?

I have no doubt that teachers are more professional and better trained than ever. Each year most of them receive tremendous amounts of training designed to help them deliver instruction in more efficient, effective ways. Much of this training involves mastering the art and science of delivering instruction in interesting and exciting ways...ways that appeal to today's students.

Here's the discouraging part: As teachers become more and more skilled in providing exciting instruction, more and more students seem chronically disinterested or bored.

Might some of this growing problem be the result of children being conditioned by 21st century life to believe that everything in life should be fast-paced, stimulating, and fun? If it weren't for the fact that many business people are struggling with this same issue, I wouldn't be so sure. Increasing numbers of employers are finding themselves having to jump through hoops to keep younger employees interested and happy on the job. A manager friend of mine put it well:

Many employees no longer believe that work should be a job... and a job should take work. They expect it to be fun, exciting, and infinitely rewarding all of the time.

What's the bottom line?

Many of us are spending far too much time, energy, and money allowing...even encouraging...our children to remain constantly involved in highly entertaining and highly stimulating activities.

Many of us are doing this because we've been led to believe that this is what "good parents" do. It's certainly true that kids benefit from participating in some entertaining activities! Unfortunately, far too many are so bombarded by them that they perceive even their most skilled and charismatic teachers as dull.

Television, Computer Games, and Other Fast-Paced Electronic Entertainment

When children have no limits over these activities, it doesn't take long before they get addicted to them...and feel bored by everything else. It shouldn't be surprising to anyone that the children who spend most of their time glued to the tube...or screen...experience the most difficulty in school.

But...who should set limits over these activities? Ideally speaking, it should be the kids...not their parents.

Before you hurl this book across the room...or call my office concerned that there's been a misprint...consider for a moment how long it will be before your kids will need the survival skill of setting limits for themselves. How long will it be before you'll need to let them out of your sight for a moment or two? How long will it be before they go off to school and encounter teachers who don't have the supernatural abilities required to make them do all of their work and learn? How long will it be before they find themselves in situations where they are tempted by their peers to do inappropriate or down-right dangerous things? How long will it be before they are driving... without you? How long will it be before they leave home and enter a world full of real and tangible life and death temptations?

It's never too early to help our children learn the survival skill of managing their own behavior! A key part of this learning involves them blowing it and experiencing the consequences of their poor decisions. As I mentioned earlier in this book, parents who understand the Love and Logic approach also understand that the "price tag" of mistakes goes up each and every day. Yes! Mistakes suffer from inflation.

I want my kids to make as many small mistakes as possible learning to manage their own behavior…so that by the time really big decisions come their way they have an extremely healthy understanding of cause and effect. Of course, this can only happen if we give them some freedom to make choices and learn from their results.

Perhaps it's time for me to share a little secret about the Love and Logic approach:

Love and Logic skills were never designed
to make kids behave.

After hearing this secret, a dad in one of my conferences blurted, "That's just great. I took the day off from work to come to this thing and hear nothing that will make my son behave."

"What you will hear," I replied, "are a number of techniques that dramatically increase the odds that he will learn how to make himself behave."

Love and Logic skills were designed
to dramatically increase the odds that kids would learn
how to make themselves behave.

The more practice our children have setting their own limits, the better they'll be at it when they are young adults…and the stakes are life and death.

Does this mean that we ought to let them run the show even when they do it poorly? No! Does all of this mean allowing them to make big mistakes that seriously affect themselves or others? Of course not! This simply means giving them *opportunities* to set limits for themselves and allowing them to make small mistakes that enable them to realize that life is better when they do a good job of controlling their own behavior. This also means being willing to step in and be far more directive if they consistently prove that they are unable to make good decisions in specific areas.

Love and Logic Experiment

A great place to start is by allowing your child to begin setting limits for themselves over television or computer games. Say the following:

Son, I thought about telling you that you couldn't have more than thirty minutes of TV or computer games per day. Then I got to thinking, "Hey, this kid of mine has a good brain! And, besides, he's going to be going out in the world in a few years and won't have me to tell him what to do." That's why I'm going to allow you to set some rules for yourself. Some days you may decide to play or watch for something like 45 minutes. Other days you might not watch or play at all. As long as I see you making good rules for yourself, I'm going to stay out of this. I love you! Good luck.

Handling the situation this way creates a successful outcome regardless of how well or poorly our children behave. If they make good decisions, they get to feel good about themselves. If they blow it, we can set limits and they can learn a critical life lesson: People who make good decisions and behave responsibly, typically get to enjoy more freedom.

NOTHING WORKS WITHOUT THE EMPATHY.

When we are forced to limit our children's freedom because of their poor decisions, what approach will create the best result? Let's consider three different parents handling this very same situation:

Parent A (with anger and sarcasm)

PARENT: "For crying-out-loud! I try to give you a little bit of responsibility, and you can't even handle it. What's wrong with you? Why don't you ever learn? That's it! No more TV! I mean it!"

SON: "Not fair! I just forgot."

PARENT: "Well, now you won't have to worry about it any-more. No TV!"

Parent B (with insecurity)

PARENT: "Didn't I tell you that you could have TV as long as you made good decisions about it?"

SON: "Not fair! I just forgot."

PARENT: "Well...okay. But I'm really getting tired of having to remind you."

Parent C (with empathy)

PARENT: "Oh, son. This is so sad. I was really hoping that you'd be able to set your own rules over the TV. Even though I really hate to do it, I guess I'll have to set the rules for you for a while. You may watch when I don't have to worry about whether or not you're getting your chores done or doing your best in school."

SON: "Not fair! I just forgot!"

PARENT: "I know...and what did I say?"

It doesn't take a parenting expert to see that the first two parents are heading for a train wreck! In early 1970s my father, Jim Fay, recognized that some parents operate a lot like drill sergeants. Like Parent A, they bark orders and often try to intimidate their kids into behaving better and making good decisions. They unintentionally send the following message:

Because you are too weak or dull to make good decisions, I'll need to tell you what to do. You're also not smart enough to learn from the consequences of your actions. That's why I need to get angry and make you feel even worse when you blow it.

My father also recognized that some parents operate a lot like helicopters on high-stakes search and rescue missions. Like Parent B, they often try to hold their kids accountable yet end up giving in and rescuing their children from the consequences of their poor decisions. Without intending to, they also send a very crippling message:

You're too weak to handle the consequences of your actions. That's why there will always be someone nearby who will make everything right for you. No sense in worrying too much about your choices. The harsh world of cause and effect does not apply to you.

My father noticed a third style of parenting that dramatically upped-the-odds of children learning to make great decisions. Like Parent C, these parents held their children accountable yet did so with love and empathy. This style, the consultant parent, sends an empowering, encouraging message:

Because you are so capable, you can learn from the natural, logical consequences of your decisions without me raising my voice, lecturing, or getting angry. Because I love you so much, I feel sad for you when you make poor decisions.

Jim and Foster chose the label "consultant" parent because these parents don't try to make their kids learn from consequences. Instead they simply allow them to experience them. Like good business consultants or mental health counselors, they understand that the problem must always remain on the shoulders of the person who created it. When a business is struggling, effective consultants don't yell at the managers or rescue them with large cash bailouts. Instead, they share ideas and take good care of themselves.

When a person is struggling with addiction, great counselors don't issue threatening lectures, and they certainly do not excuse their client from the consequences of their drug habit. Instead, they provide compassion, share helpful ideas, and remember to maintain healthy boundaries.

Great parents also maintain "healthy boundaries" by remembering that children must own the problems they create. How else will they learn from the consequences of these problems?

You already know the very most powerful tool for maintaining solid boundaries:

Provide empathy and allow consequences to do the teaching.

When we become angry, it makes the child's problem ours. Obviously rescuing ends in the same result.

Only when we give some freedom…show compassion and understanding when they make poor decisions…will our children learn to handle serious responsibilities.

Isn't it freeing to know that you don't have to make your kids learn from their poor decisions? Isn't it a relief to know that empathy and consequences will do the teaching for you? Isn't it comforting to know that you can be relaxed and loving instead of having to display anger or having to give endless lectures?

Isn't it also interesting that freedom and responsibility always go hand in hand? Kids can't learn responsibility without being given the freedom to make mistakes and to learn from them. Children will never learn how to handle freedom without first learning responsibility…and this responsibility is never an easy thing to learn.

Many *adults* find it difficult to set limits with themselves over TV, computer games, etc. That's why we shouldn't be surprised if our kids have a hard time also. The main thing is that we remain actively involved in their lives so that we can step in and temporarily limit their freedom as a logical consequence for poor decision-making.

As time passes, and they grow and mature, we're also wise to return some of this freedom so that they have additional opportunities to learn. If we make the mistake of pulling back and never giving them another chance, they'll never come to realize that they are capable human beings who can learn from their mistakes.

Love and Logic Experiment

As we all know, kids need plenty of practice making decisions…so that they'll eventually become decision-making black belts, capable of protecting themselves in a temptation-laden world. This is why it's important to give them additional opportunities to practice with freedom as time goes by. When you think that your child may be ready for another learning opportunity, pat them on the back and say:

This is so exciting! A few months ago, you had a hard time making rules for yourself about your computer games. I'm thinking that you've become a lot more grown up in a lot of ways. I think it's time for you to try setting rules for yourself again. I'll stay out of it as long as I see you doing a good job. Good luck!

Some Important Cautions about Computers, Video Games, and Cell Phones

There is no substitute for direct parental supervision of these activities! Don't make the mistake of thinking that electronic blocking devices are a substitute for actually reviewing what your kids are doing with their computers, video game players, cell phones, and other electronic devices.

While there is nothing inherently wrong with youngsters having such devices, they need to be regarded as privileges rather than needs…luxuries rather than necessities. Understanding this gives us the guts to take them away if our kids prove unwilling to set limits over their own behavior. Understanding this also enables us to extinguish the verbal arrows they send our way when we set limits:

"But it's educational!"

Don't you love this one! I even tried this on my parents, trying to convince them that watching *The Monkees* or *Gilligan's Island* on TV would somehow boost my scholastic abilities. Nowadays many parents seem to fall for this one when it comes to their children's use of the World Wide Web. If your child really needs to use the internet for educational purposes, they should have no problem allowing you to supervise what they are doing.

Love and Logic Experiment

When your child complains, "But it's educational!" reply with sweet enthusiasm:

That's great! Since it's educational, I'd like to learn along with you. Feel free to be on the Web as long as I can enjoy what you are learning, too.

Of course, this won't make your kids want to hug you, but it's a great way to set limits. When they continue to complain, repeat with great empathy:

I love you too much to argue about this.

"But I'll need it just in case there's a terrorist attack!"
After September 11th, 2001 many kids have grabbed onto this
one and used it to hold their parents hostage. I'm unaware of any
potential terrorist attack thwarted by a teenager with a cell phone.
While I wish it were true, a cell phone cannot be used to shield
oneself from bullets or bombs.

To be fair, cell phones are wonderful devices that can keep us and
our kids safe. Unfortunately, they frequently become more damaging
than protective. When our children are sending sexually provocative
texts or pictures to each other, is the potentially protective value
of this device worth the massive damage it is doing to their souls?
When they spend more time texting than paying attention to their
teachers, are their cell phones really keeping them safe?

Love and Logic Experiment
If your child uses the "but I need it for safety" manipulation
strategy, fill your voice with love and say:

*Won't it be great when you're able to do that? You may have
your phone for safety when I can see that you are making good
decisions about other things in your life and prove to me that
you can benefit from it.*

If your youngster gets really mad about this limit, pat yourself
on the back for being a good parent!

---

*There is nothing that will keep our kids safe if we are not
teaching them that each and every one of their decisions
has potentially serious, life-altering consequences.*

When kids use cell phones for exclusively good and noble purposes, they get the added benefit of being a bit safer because they have them.

"But all of my friends get to..!"

This…too…is an age-old manipulation strategy.

Love and Logic Experiment

When your child says, "Yeah, but all of my friends…"

Just repeat:

I love you too much to argue.

Have you ever noticed that the fewer words you use in these situations, the more effective you become?

The very most important limit we can set over computers and internet use is to expect that the computer be placed some place where we can keep an eye on it…not in our child's room! Because the stakes are so high, this is one limit I don't recommend allowing kids to set for themselves. Remember: People who apply the Love and Logic philosophy hope and pray that youngsters will make *affordable* mistakes. "Chatting" with a pedophile on their computer is NOT an affordable mistake. Surfing the internet and getting hooked on porn sites isn't either. Neither is getting so addicted to games that real life…and real people…always take a back seat.

"But you don't trust me!"

I actually like it when kids say this. Why? Simply because it opens the door for me to be completely honest with them and say, "You're right."

Okay, don't get me wrong here. I'm not trying to be a smart alec...or something else like one. What I'm trying to communicate is that I don't trust anybody when it comes to unmonitored internet use. I've been around far too many good adults who've gotten themselves caught up in really bad stuff on the Web. If adults have a hard time handling this new, intensely tempting technology, what makes us think that our kids should be able to handle it without caring and consistent supervision and guidance?

Love and Logic Experiment to do right away...

IF YOUR CHILD'S COMPUTER IS IN THEIR ROOM OR SOME OTHER PLACE BEHIND CLOSED DOORS, REMOVE IT IMMEDIATELY! PUT IT IN A COMMON AREA SOME PLACE WHERE YOU CAN KEEP A CLOSE EYE ON IT.

Something else you can do...

When your child says, "You don't trust me!" remember your empathy and say:

I don't even trust myself when it comes to the computer. That's why I make sure that your mom can always see my history and my emails. Lots of adults have a really difficult time not getting pulled into bad things on their computers. I guess this is one of those things in life where it's best to have the people who love you help you stay out of trouble.

You might even add:

Oh...by the way...if you ever want to check my computer, feel free to. I always appreciate feeling like people love me enough to help me stay out of trouble.

Extracurricular Activities

Can too many healthy extracurricular activities, such as music, sports, etc., also create kids who experience chronic boredom in school? You bet! Generally speaking, extracurricular activities are good for kids! In fact, there's a growing body of research suggesting that involvement in these activities improves academic achievement and helps kids resist involvement in drugs, alcohol, sex, and other high-risk activities. I suppose it makes sense that the better kids feel about themselves, the better they'll do in school...and the less likely they'll need to "self-medicate."

These activities become a liability when they become so numerous and time-consuming that they interfere with downtime, chores, and the simple joys of life. Yes! Kids need downtime. Adults need downtime. When our lives become nothing more than a blur of activity, we run the risk of creating kids who aren't willing to take the time to think and learn. When this begins to happen, their minds fixate so deeply on all of these exciting activities that their teachers become an annoying distraction...an irritating background noise.

When our lives become nothing more than a blur of activity, we run the risk of creating kids who aren't willing to take the time to think and learn.

Over the past few decades, many have begun to believe that we're doing kids a grave disservice if we aren't getting them involved in as many extracurricular activities as possible. Factor in the "keeping up with the Joneses" phenomenon, and we've got a lot of kids who are involved in way too many activities.

If this strikes a nerve...if it seems all too familiar...maybe it's time for limits. Again, we encourage parents to give their children an opportunity to set these limits. Again, this requires that children are given a healthy dose of freedom...along with the responsibility that must always accompany this freedom.

Love and Logic Experiment

If you are concerned that your child might be overscheduled, encourage him to begin setting some limits:

Honey, I'm a bit concerned that you've gotten yourself involved in way too many activities. Since you inherited my amazing intellectual ability, I really think that you are smart enough to make some good decisions about how much you can handle without it continuing to get in the way of school, your chores, or your health. If you want any ideas, let me know. I love you!

As the Love and Logic philosophy teaches, problems are best solved by the people who have them. It also teaches that our job is to give some guidance, provide empathy when things go poorly, and allow consequences to do the teaching.

Many parents are amazed by the great decisions their children make when they empower them in this way. One dad relayed, "If I would have gone to my daughter and told her that she had to drop one of her activities, we would have had World War III on our hands. When I handed her the problem, she came to me five days later and asked me for advice about how to talk with her Tae Kwon Do coach about taking a break from his classes!"

As any seasoned parent understands, sometimes things work...and sometimes they don't. Either way, our children are given the gift of learning important life lessons about freedom and responsibility.

Love and Logic Experiment

If your child fails to make good decisions, help her learn from her mistakes by setting and enforcing progressively tighter limits:

Oh, honey. This isn't good. We're seeing that you are still so busy with all of your friends and your activities that you don't have enough time to think about school and about keeping up with your chores. Unfortunately, when you don't set good limits for yourself we have to set the limits. It's time for you to make some tough decisions about which activities you really want to keep participating in. We'd like for you to make those decisions... but we'll make them if you don't. We know this is really hard. We love you!

NOTHING WORKS WITHOUT THE EMPATHY.

Show Them How it Looks

I'm just as guilty as anybody of showing my kids how to live a hectic, fast-paced life. The older I get, the more I realize how destructive this is.

The grayer I get, the more I'm convinced that all this insanity accomplishes is the creation of more kids who're easily bored and more difficult to motivate. As you've probably noticed, this also creates parents who are stressed and tired all of the time!

One of the toughest things I've had to face is admitting that keeping busy is just one of the ways I avoid dealing with the underlying hurts in my life. Without getting too personal, I have some hurts. Now that I think about it, the people next door have some hurts. Oh…and the lady who cuts my hair has some hurts. I suppose it's safe to say that just about everybody has at least one emotional hurt.

Hurts are part of life. What creates the big problems for most of us are not so much our hurts but the hurtful ways we try to deal with our hurts. The dangerous thing about using busyness to mask our pain or discomfort is that our fast-paced culture leaves us thinking that this is how everyone is supposed to behave. Like hamsters running on exercise wheels, we look at each other and reason, "Joe next to me…and Mary on the other side…they're spinning their wheels just like me. Ah, all is right with the world."

Like hamsters running in exercise wheels,
we look at each other and reason, "Joe next to me…
and Mary on the other side…they're spinning their wheels
just like me. Ah, all is right with the world."

If this doesn't apply to you don't give it another thought.

Some things that you can do…

If you think it might…and you can see the connection it has with raising kids who view their teachers as archaic 80s-era computers, it's never too late to start making some changes:

- Give yourself permission to turn your cell phone off during family times.
- Consider asking them to do the same. (It really is okay to set some limits designed to help them learn that using the phone during meals or other family times is rude.)
- Make at least one day of the week a TV-off/computer-off day.
- Let them see you reading a book after dinner.
- Take the time each day to look into their eyes and remember their gifts.
- Enjoy some quiet times together.
- If you just can't seem to slow down, ask yourself, "Are there any hurts in my life I'm using all of this busyness to avoid? Do I need some help learning healthier ways of dealing with these hurts?"

Your Kids Will Experience Withdrawal

The last time I had a real vacation I just about went nuts. Before we got there, the thought of spending an entire week on the beach in Florida sounded amazing. About three hours into the first day I was crawling out of my skin, wondering if there was some way I could rent a laptop without my wife finding out. Would she notice if I got a really big beach blanket and hid under it as I answered an email or two?

As that wonderful week neared its end, I began to relax and enjoy myself. As I did, I realized that my mind and my body had become addicted to constant activity, stress, and chaos. Going cold turkey was the only thing that shocked me into the realization that many of us are so addicted to craziness that we'll do anything to get a fix. Might this also give us some insight regarding why many children react so adversely when we begin to expect them to slow down?

If you decide to take some of this advice...and your kids get really upset, argue, and complain...you can take comfort in the fact that they are normal. If they whine about being bored, you can pat yourself on the back, knowing that you are giving them a great gift. If they accuse you of being a Neanderthal or of being "like so five minutes ago" simply repeat, "I love you too much to argue."

> ***If you decide to take some of this advice...***
> ***and your kids get really upset, argue, and complain...***
> ***you can take comfort in the fact that***
> ***they are normal.***

My parents gave me a wonderful gift every summer...lots of chores and not much excitement. Sure...summers were nice at first...but it really got old by the end of June. As clear as yesterday I remember being nine and sitting on the front steps next to my best friend, Randy:

"There's nothing to doooo," I complained.

Nodding, he mumbled, "Yeah...boring."

Without thinking I uttered words that hung in the air like the smell of dirty socks in a gym bag: "Yeah...it'd be better to be in schoooool."

What self-respecting boy of nine would admit such a thing? Only one with parents wise enough to understand that we do kids no favors when we provide nonstop activity, excitement, and entertainment.

Your Child Can Succeed!

Allow them to believe this by allowing them to struggle.

"I don't want my kids to struggle like I did."

What a noble and loving desire! This age-old hope…shared by countless caring parents…has its pros and cons. On the upside, it motivates the loving and wise to shield their children from overwhelming hardships and struggles. Obviously, no good can come from youngsters becoming so discouraged or traumatized that they give up on life. On the downside, this hope can at times motivate us to take away the struggles or hardships necessary for the development of solid character, coping skills, and happiness.

The processes of refining gold and of tempering steel come to mind. Each requires extreme heat. To separate gold from surrounding impurities, the raw material must be heated to approximate 1,100 degrees Celsius. To harden steel requires exposing the unfinished product to temperatures ranging from 150 to 500 degrees Celsius.

For our children to develop precious, gold-like character…as well as the strength to endure life's challenges…they also need to be subjected to some heat. Daily struggles, such as completing chores, coping with boredom in the grocery store, solving problems with their teachers, dealing with peer or sibling conflicts, learning challenging academic content, experiencing the consequences of their poor decisions, etc., are all critical for the development of this strength and character. Children only develop a can-do attitude and happiness when they're expected to struggle with hardship… and when they see that they have what it takes to cope.

Can you see the connection between struggle and academic motivation?

Children who are never expected to struggle at home rarely believe that they should be required to struggle at school. They also tend to be extremely unhappy kids!

Love and Logic Experiment

The next time you see your child struggling with something they are working on, resist the urge to tell them what to do or do it for them. If they ask for help, give them ideas but do your best to allow them the satisfaction of doing most of the work.

Remember that children who are never allowed to work through the challenges they encounter come to believe that they are weak and incapable. These feelings of incompetence fuel academic underachievement like coal fires a furnace.

Are educators seeing ever increasing numbers of children who believe it a violation of their civil liberties to have a teacher expect them to do something challenging? Are employers also seeing more and more adult employees who believe the same?

Are educators witnessing elevated numbers of students who think so little of their own abilities that they shrink from any challenging task? Are employers observing escalating numbers of adults who suffer from this same sort of emotional paralysis?

Like stink on a skunk, a sense of entitlement, unhappiness, and academic underachievement go hand in hand. Chances aren't good for the survival of America if we as a country continue to create more and more children with this triad of apathy.

> *Like stink on a skunk,*
> *a sense of entitlement, unhappiness,*
> *and academic underachievement*
> *go hand in hand.*

On the flip side, parents who teach their children how to manage adversity create kids who enjoy a tremendous advantage over their apathetic peers! Wouldn't it be wonderful to give your kids the gift of knowing that when the going gets tough, they've got what it takes to keep going? Besides knowing that you love them unconditionally, there's nothing more precious than teaching your children that...

- Happiness and success aren't free.
- Happiness and success require hard work.
- Happiness and success are usually earned by overcoming hardships.
- Happy and successful people are simply willing to struggle more frequently than their less content and less successful peers.

Over the last three decades we've discovered a practical and very powerful process for fostering these attitudes:

Risk Made Possible Through Relationship

Struggle

Encouragement

Hard-Earned Success

Self-Respect, Motivation, and Happiness

Risk Made Possible Through Relationship

Without risk there's no reward. The type of "risk" I'm talking about here does not involve playing in traffic, hang-gliding off skyscrapers, experimenting with drugs, etc. Instead, examples of the "healthy risks" that build healthy self-efficacy involve struggling to...

- Tie your shoes all by yourself.
- Read new words that look really big.
- Finish your science fair project mostly without help from your dad.
- Talk to your teacher about a problem without your parent doing it for you.
- Tell the waiter what you would like to eat instead of having your mom do it for you.
- Fix your own sack lunch for school.
- Make friends with new kids at school.

- Do some math problems that look really scary.
- Present a speech in front of your classmates.
- Move out of the house when you become an adult…instead of mooching off your parents for the rest of your life.

What leaves *you* feeling the proudest and most motivated? Is it doing something that appears simple and nonthreatening? Not typically.

There's no arguing that the greatest feelings of excitement and pride come from accomplishments that initially appear intimidating or overwhelming. Overcoming the tough stuff gives our youngsters the greatest gifts of satisfaction, security, and happiness!

Isn't it sad when we as parents or educators steal the struggle? Few of us start each day with a written plan for doing so. Nevertheless, it's easy to slip into the trap of unintentionally removing too many healthy risks from children's lives. Because we love them and want them to be happy, it can be difficult to remember the following:

Children have to experience some frustration
and be upset in the short-term to develop motivation
and happiness in the long-term.

Now…how do we up the odds of children actually being willing to try things that they perceive as too difficult or threatening? That's where the rubber really hits the pavement!

RELATIONSHIP!

Are you more willing to try things for people who leave you feeling anxious and inadequate? Or are you far more willing to risk for those who leave you feeling loved and secure? Are you more willing to risk for people who fly off the handle when you make a mistake? Or are you far more likely to take risks around folks who love you even when you blow it big time?

> *Unconditional love and acceptance*
> *is the magic that allows children*
> *to take the sorts of healthy risks required*
> *for the development of motivation*
> *and happiness.*

Perhaps the biggest step we can take toward creating homes where children are willing to take healthy risks involves assessing our own beliefs about whether it's okay for our children to mess up. Here we go again! Here we are…right back to the topic of children making mistakes. Are you thinking that I like it when children make small blunders? Are you thinking that this represents a critical part of the Love and Logic approach to raising self-assured, motivated, responsible kids?

Far more importantly, do YOU *really* believe that it's good for kids to make some mistakes?

Or…is it possible that you and your children are imprisoned by worry that even small blunders will doom their chances of happiness and success? Fear of mistakes can act as a personal terrorist in our lives, creeping into our hearts and minds and insidiously holding us and our children hostage to hopelessness.

How we feel about error will heavily affect whether our children believe it's okay to take the risks required to learn and grow…or come to believe that it's better to play it safe and give up before there's any possibility of error.

Fear of mistakes can act as a personal terrorist in our lives, creeping into our hearts and minds and insidiously holding us and our children hostage to hopelessness.

The freedom to make affordable mistakes equals the freedom to learn and grow toward one's true potential. When we begin to internalize this belief system…when we begin to make this paradigm shift…it opens the door for creating homes (and classrooms) where children feel free to learn and grow.

Love and Logic Experiment

Some parents just can't seem to stomach the thought of their children taking "risks" or making "mistakes." Many of these same parents find it far more palatable for their children to run plenty of "experiments." Listed below are just a few of the wonderful scientific research opportunities available to our youngsters. Consider this list and ask yourself, "What additional research projects do my kids need to be involved in?"

- Deciding to play instead of finishing their math homework.
- "Forgetting" to do their chores.
- Doing their homework all by themselves…without you making sure that it is correct.
- Waiting until the last moment to begin work on their science fair project.
- Sitting next to a friend at school who might distract them from doing their work.
- Spending all of their own money on one item that they don't need.

As I already mentioned, the "price tag" of "research projects" goes up every day. Wouldn't it be wonderful if your kids conducted so many when they were young that they had Ph.D.'s in wisdom by the time they became adults?

Love and Logic Experiment

What should we do when the "experiments" our kids want to make have potentially serious consequences for themselves or others?

Forget about the Love and Logic philosophy…or any other parenting philosophy.

Do whatever is within your power to stop them.

Even though common sense has been outlawed for use in Washington, D.C., we can continue to apply it in our homes.

(Oh…and I'm not just picking on one political party here.)

When we begin to embrace the notion that the road to wisdom is paved with mistakes, we begin to relate far differently to our kids. Instead of coming across to them as stressed and anxious, we interact with them in a far more relaxed and joyful way. Instead of sending "This is probably too tough for you" messages, we begin to send ones that communicate, "You can handle this!" Instead of fretting that things will go wrong, we often find ourselves hoping that they will. Instead of flying off the handle when mistakes are made, we find ourselves in a far better state of mind to express love and sincere empathy.

Consider for a moment how you might operate around two different types of bosses:

Mr. Boundupshorts, Boss A, throws a fit every time you...or anybody else...makes a mistake.

Mr. Softboxers, Boss B, keeps his cool. Instead of yelling, lecturing, or threatening, he calmly asks, "So...what have you learned from that?"

Old Boundupshorts's goal is to make sure that you "pay" for the mistakes you make.

Softboxers is more concerned that you've learned something from your mistake.

Boundupshorts thinks that you have to feel horrible in order to learn.

Softboxers understands that people are far more likely to learn from mistakes when they aren't distracted by anger, frustration, or their own fear.

One boss creates a company where employees are afraid to think, take reasonable risks, and grow. The other creates a firm where folks aren't afraid to be creative. One boss creates a workplace where employees begin to feel incapable. The other creates an environment where they feel empowered. One boss probably has a lot of employees who engage in all sort of passive-resistant behaviors, such as working a bit slower, coming back from breaks just a bit late, "losing" paperwork, and treating customers the same way they are treated by their boss. The other enjoys intense loyalty, respect, and hard work from his employees.

Which boss would you rather work for?

The type of relationship we have with our children is largely determined by how we react when the rubber hits the pavement...and they blow it big time. In essence, it is at these difficult times that we have the opportunity to show our kids that we either believe in their abilities...or that we don't. It's also during these times that we have the chance to prove to our children that we will love them no matter what.

Empathy is the key!

NOTHING WORKS WITHOUT THE EMPATHY.

Love and Logic Experiment

Don't be afraid to let your kids see you make mistakes. That is as long as you're not getting angry and frustrated with yourself for making them.

If they see us beating ourselves up over our errors, they'll learn to do the same. If, instead, they witness us viewing goofs as golden learning opportunities, they'll be far less fearful of failure.

The next time you make a mistake, allow your kids to overhear you saying something like:

Uh, oh.... That didn't go well. Well...the good thing about mistakes is that you get to learn from them. The next time I'm going to _____ .

---

*The type of relationship we have with our children
is largely determined by how we react when
the rubber hits the pavement...and they blow it big time.*

Struggle

For many of us it's tough to sit back and allow our kids to grapple
with challenging tasks. I'm constantly fighting the urge to do
things for my kids that they can really do for themselves. Years
ago one of my sons, Marc, decided that he wanted to hike to the
top of a big hill near our home. Since he was only four at the time,
I figured that I'd end up having to carry him most of the way.
Have you ever gone on a hike with a four-year-old? They have a
two-speed transmission: warp speed and park. Within the first ten
minutes, he was already complaining about how hard it was...and
how tired he was...and how he was *dying* of thirst. Fortunately,
something inside me whispered, "Let him struggle through this.
Let him do this without making it too easy. Don't take this away
from him." After much encouraging on my part, he finally made it
to the top...under his own power! The smile on his face was price-
less! So is the fact that he still talks with pride about this accomplishment...even though it was nearly fourteen years ago!

By the way...I carried him down the hill.

As I see it, great parenting is a bit like tightrope walking. With
every move, we're carefully paying attention to the relationship
between our child's abilities and the challenges facing them. When
it looks like these hardships won't overwhelm their capabilities,
we allow them to struggle and provide loving guidance. When the
task is clearly too difficult or dangerous we step in to prevent them
from becoming permanently discouraged...or injured.

> ***When it looks like hardships***
> ***won't overwhelm their capabilities,***
> ***allow them to struggle and provide***
> ***loving guidance.***

Isn't parenting a humbling adventure?

Encouragement

We all know that kids need encouragement as they struggle. Unfortunately, many people find it difficult to give this encouragement. Generally speaking, these are the folks who never received this gift from their own parents. I'm often amazed and saddened by the number of people I meet who were raised with constant criticism and put-downs. Most of the time their parents were doing what they thought was best…giving plenty of "corrective feedback."

Have you ever been around someone who gave you plenty of this "corrective feedback"? Is it highly motivating, or does it get old really quick?

> ***There is nothing more demotivating than***
> ***a constant diet of corrective feedback.***

People are far more motivated to learn and improve when most of our energy is focused on what they are doing well. When children are struggling with difficult tasks they need to hear things like…

- "I know this is challenging, and here is what I see you doing well…"
- "I've noticed that when you keep trying you can do just about anything."

- "How proud of yourself will you be when you finish this?"
- "Should you be proud of yourself for doing something that's this tough?"
- "It makes me happy for you to see that you aren't afraid to try things that are hard."

I'm often asked, "What can I say when my child says, 'I can't do it' or 'It's too hard' or 'I'm stupid'?" Here's my advice: Smile, pat the child on the back and ask, "Aren't you glad that I don't believe that?" Simply asking the question communicates that you believe in them…and that you aren't going to get into a back-and-forth argument over whether or not they're capable.

> *When a child says "I'm stupid" reply,*
> *"Aren't you glad that I don't*
> *believe that?"*

Hard-Earned Success

There is nothing more motivating than success…particularly when success is hard- earned. When we build relationships that make it safe for kids to take healthy risks, encourage and guide them along the way, and allow them to see themselves being successful, the foundation for academic achievement motivation is strengthened.

The key is allowing kids to contribute the lion's share of the work required for this success. Too frequently, we as adults contribute well over 50% of the effort in an attempt to help children experience success. Instead of giving suggestions, encouraging, and stepping in only when necessary, we either tell the child exactly what to do at each and every step…or we just do most of it for them. This tendency has become so pervasive in modern day America that it may be time to change the name of the elementary school science fair to the "Adult Skills Expo."

Are you working harder on your children's success than they are?

There is nothing more motivating than success…
particularly when success is hard-earned.

A powerful strategy for avoiding this trap is getting into the habit of asking guiding questions, rather than telling kids what to do.

Love and Logic Experiment

The next time you witness your child working on something really challenging, experiment with asking questions instead of making statements. Questions imply confidence in their abilities and allow us to guide them toward success without doing too much of the work. Examples include:

- "Do you think that you need to put your shoelace through this hole or this one?"
- "Have you ever thought about paying close attention to how other kids make friends?"
- "Does the decimal point go here? Or does it go here?"
- "Does it work best to complain about being bored? Or does it work better to find something you can do to help yourself feel better?"
- "Is the tag on your shirt supposed to go in the front?"
- "What do you think you could do so that you don't miss the bus in the morning?"

When we prompt thinking with questions, it allows children to move toward success while continuing to take plenty of credit for it. Questions also promote thinking while reducing resistance.

Self-Respect, Motivation, and Happiness (The Magic Coat)

In my presentations, I often provide an example of a nine-year-old boy whose mother cured him of Responsibility Deficit Disorder (RDD). She'd previously been a hard core "helicopter parent." After learning some Love and Logic concepts, she realized that all of her hovering and rescuing wasn't helping. "Perhaps," she began to wonder, "I've been stealing the struggle."

Bursting through the door one afternoon, he whined, "Somebody stole my coat!" Since he'd lost approximately 2.5 coats per school year, she wasn't surprised. In the past she'd responded with lectures, guilt, and a brand new coat...one that was far nicer than the one he'd lost. This time she locked in the empathy and asked him how he was planning to buy himself another. He wasn't impressed with her newly acquired parenting prowess. But...nevertheless...he decided that purchasing a used coat at the thrift store was within his means. Mom commented:

> *He was so mad at me at first! Then I noticed something strange. As soon as he put on that ratty old coat, he grew about a foot. For the next four months, he strutted around, proclaiming to everyone how he had bought it, all by himself. It wasn't long before I realized that the worn-out three-dollar coat was a greater gift to him than all of the expensive birthday and Christmas presents he'd received during his lifetime. That worn-out coat was a magic coat that made him feel bigger than anything I could have ever done for him.*

Is there any gift greater than self-respect? Is there any gift greater than knowing that you've got what it takes to make it through the tough times? Does true motivation and happiness come from having an easy life...or one filled with some manageable hardships and loving, encouraging people?

Your Child Can Make a Difference in the World!

*Kids who have a purpose in life
are far more likely to find a purpose in school.*

Humans have such a strong need for purpose in their lives that they will do almost anything to get it met. This striving for purpose… this need to be needed…this yearning to contribute can serve as an immensely powerful and positive motivator. That is, as long as we nurture it by guiding our children toward understanding that the key to meeting it involves serving…rather than being served.

A quick glance at two very different individuals may serve to illuminate this concept. Perhaps you've met one like the first. I'll call him Oscar.

Oscar is a proud member of the "Me" generation. "What's in this for me?" is his motto. All's right with the world…according to Oscar…as long as the planet is kissing his posterior. Yep! As long as he has the car he wants, the house he desires, a wife who behaves the way he wants, etc., he's motivated and happy. Does Oscar have a purpose? Sure! To make sure Oscar's life is as easy and comfortable as possible.

Despite his constant striving, Oscar is never very content. No matter how well things are going for him, he'll never experience joy. He'll either spend his time being angry about not having enough or spinning his wheels in pursuit of bigger and better thrills. No matter how well-fed he is, he'll forever feel empty.

Chances are pretty good that you've also met someone like Bill.

Sure, Bill likes nice stuff. Sure he likes it when people do what he wants. The difference between Bill and Oscar is that Bill spends the lion's share of his time thinking, "What can I do to make this world a better place?"

Without a doubt, Bill's sense of purpose is far more solid and gratifying than Oscar's. Regardless of whether life serves him sweet grapes or sour apples, Bill has the enduring hope that his time of earth will in some way ease the load of others. Bill doesn't have to rely on everything going well to feel content. His happiness is not dependent upon what others do. Instead, it's dependent upon his enduring sense of purpose.

Some questions to ponder...
- Which of these men best personify the attitudes you desire for your kids?
- Which set of attitudes best equips children for academic success?
- Which set of attitudes gives youngsters the best shot at success in life?
- Which set of attitudes best allows your children to remain positive even when they experience setbacks?
- Which set of beliefs leaves people with the fewest regrets as they near the sunset of their lives?

Clearly our friend, Bill, best personifies what most of us want for our children. That's why it's so critically important for them to develop a sense of purpose as early in their lives as possible. Boiled down to its most basic form, this perspective comes from growing up in a family where they feel needed, depended upon, and inspired by their parents' example of generosity toward others.

Perhaps the first question to ask is:

Do my kids feel like needed and valued members of our family team or "gang"?

In chapter four, I nailed down the idea that children need meaningful chores to experience this feeling. Reading this chapter, you'll see the intimate connection between growing up as a family team member and becoming a highly motivated societal team member. Of course, chores aren't the only way to give children this gift. Other duties…not traditionally viewed as "chores" are equally valuable.

A wonderful teacher, known for bringing the best out of troubled students, had this rule for himself:

If a child can do it…a child should do it.

On a daily basis he reminded himself that doing too much for his students robs them of opportunities to experience a true sense of purpose. It also robs them of the excitement and motivation of believing that they have valuable contributions to make. Remembering these truths, he made sure that each of his students had key responsibilities, such as helping other students when they were struggling, tutoring younger children, helping new students feel comfortable, helping other school staff with important jobs, etc. Soon after adopting this practice, he began to notice that his students were far happier and more motivated team players. He also noticed that he was spending a lot less time dealing with bad behavior.

Take this principle into your home, and you'll raise happier, more responsible, and far more motivated kids!

Love and Logic Experiment

Create a list titled "Other Ways to Help My Kids Feel Needed." Examples include:

- Preparing and cleaning up after at least one family meal per week.
- Checking the newspaper for coupons so that the family can save money.
- Helping younger siblings with homework or school projects.
- Helping at the grocery store by making sure that everything on the list is purchased.
- Helping their younger siblings get ready in the morning.
- Helping neighbors by shoveling snow or other jobs.

Does it light a motivational fire under your seat when you feel unimportant and believe that your contributions are unneeded?

Or...do you feel far more enthusiastic and motivated when you know that people are truly depending upon you to come through for them?

How important is a sense of purpose?

Motivated by the horrific experiences he endured as a Nazi death camp survivor, Viktor Frankl wrote his book *Man's Search for Meaning*. In it he discussed how an enduring sense of meaning…or purpose…made it possible for him and many others to survive. Asked about the attainment of happiness and success, Frankl commented:

"Don't aim at success. The more you aim at it and make it a target, the more you are going to miss it. For success, like happiness, cannot be pursued; it must ensue, and it only does so as the unintended side-effect of one's personal dedication to a cause greater than oneself or as the by-product of one's surrender to a person other than oneself."

Love and Logic Experiment

As often as possible allow your kids to overhear you talking about your sense of purpose…what you do that serves others.

You've probably already discovered that children tend to learn far more from what they overhear than what they are told. Take advantage of this truth by letting them overhear you talking about how much satisfaction you derive from helping others.

The "Purpose-Achievement" Connection

Which child will be the most motivated to achieve in school when the subject matter becomes difficult, a bit boring, or downright tedious? Will it be the child without a strong sense of purpose, or will it be the one who's been taught to believe that they can and will make a difference in the world?

For decades, educational experts have urged teachers to make their lessons more relevant and meaningful to students. Without a doubt, children are more likely to be motivated when they can see how the information presented applies to improving the quality of their lives. Nevertheless, the teacher's role in establishing relevance is only half of the equation. What about the student's role? If children are never taught to find meaning in their lives, will educators ever be successful in ensuring that they find meaning in school?

The Deceptiveness of "Me Psychology"

Has modern pop psychology actually contributed to this problem?

Over the past fifty or so years, popular psychology has been dominated by the goal of helping people feel good about themselves. While a noble goal, this emphasis on *personal* growth and *personal* fulfillment has led many down a *personal* path toward emptiness. By allowing their clients to obsess over *personal* problems, as well as how to get their own *personal* wants met, too many well-meaning therapists have failed to help their clients realize the freedom and joy that comes from also tending to the needs of others. Many of these "helping professionals" have quite successfully assisted their clients in "getting in touch with their inner children." The problem...as I see it...is that folks who are too cozy with their "inner children" fail to outgrow the selfish characteristics of small children.

Now...let me give credit to all of those wonderful psychologists, therapists, counselors, social workers, etc., who haven't followed this path! Please hear me loud and clear! My intention is NOT to bash all mental health professionals. I DO NOT want to discourage people from seeking needed and effective therapy!

I DO want to encourage those in need to find well-trained professionals who will help them discover the therapeutic nature of moving outside of selfish desires and placing one's focus on others who are needful.

***Folks who are too cozy with their "inner children"
fail to outgrow the selfish characteristics of small children.***

About forty years ago, "me psychology" began to leap the boundary between the therapist's couch and the public school classroom. Although a large number of educators have resisted this unhealthy trend, those who haven't believe that it is their job to make certain that students are shielded from any sort of struggle, inconvenience, or failure. This very vocal minority has probably influenced educational practice more than we realize. Evidence of their impact can be seen in the following policies seen in some schools:

• Teachers must grade papers with green ink rather than red. Green, of course, is a much gentler color.
• Failure is not an option. If a student does poorly, they must be allowed to redo the work as many times as necessary to get a good grade.
• It is the teacher's job to make sure each student learns. (When I was a child, it was my job to make sure that I learned!)
• Parents at home are solely responsible for making sure that their children do their homework. (When I was a child, it was my job to be responsible about getting it done!)
• Because children have been known to hurt each other's feelings, we should abolish the archaic practice of recess...or any other activity where kids are allowed to freely interact with each other without constant adult micromanagement.

So…why have I spent so much ink on the perils of "me psychology"? Four reasons:

First

It has led many to believe that being a "good parent" or "good educator" means *serving* children so that they will be comfortable, content, and successful all of the time.

Second

This has led many children to believe that they should be *served* all of the time…so that they are always comfortable, content, and successful.

Third

This has made it incredibly tough for many compassionate educators and parents who believe that children need to be treated with great love…while at the same time held to high standards and taught that they are not the center of the universe.

Fourth

All of this has culminated in creating vast numbers of children… and adults…perpetually imprisoned by feelings of entitlement and unhappiness.

Is it really so wise to make our children the center of attention all of the time?

Don't we already have enough Narcissistic Personality Disordered people?

Love and Logic Experiment

Don't allow your kids to interrupt you when you are talking with others. This unfortunate habit on the part of many adults has led far too many children to believe that their wants are far more important than the needs of others.

Experiment with calmly yet firmly saying:

I will be happy to listen when we are done talking.

If your child continues to interrupt, say:

This is really sad. You're really draining my energy.

When it's convenient for you, your child can replace this energy by doing extra chores, staying home instead of being driven some place they want to go, hiring their own babysitter so that you can go out for a calm quiet meal, etc.

And remember…deliver this consequence with empathy instead of anger.

NOTHING WORKS WITHOUT THE EMPATHY.

Will your children thank you for helping them realize that they aren't the true center of the universe? Will they congratulate you on your effort to give them the gift of purpose? Of course not! That is…they probably won't until they grow older and begin to realize that their lives are more content as a result.

Will you receive medals from all of the adults around you? Or…
is it more probable that some will view you as being too demanding,
old-fashioned, or mean? Unfortunately, there are plenty of adults in
just about every family, neighborhood, or school who believe that
children should be worshipped and served as idols…rather than be
loved and guided toward becoming respectful and responsible.

Be brave my friend! Those courageous enough to give children
the gift of selflessness need a thick skin! When the going gets
tough, maybe it'll help to remember the following:

*Those absorbed with self are typically absorbed
with unhappiness and burnout.*

*Those absorbed with making the world a better place
are absorbed with excitement and enthusiasm.*

Can *you* find a purpose in *your* life?

Some worry that because they aren't doctors, scientists, social workers,
preachers, or politicians, there's no way they can model a sense of
purpose for their children. They may even find themselves thinking,
"How do I find any meaning in this lousy job or this lousy life?"

If Viktor Frankl could find meaning in his atrocious Nazi death
camp experience, is there hope for anyone? Clear as day from his
powerful life experience is the truth that purpose can be found
regardless of one's life circumstances. Purpose is an internal condition…rather than an external one.

I often find myself thinking of our garbage collector. Every week
he smiles, waves, and says "hello" as he tosses our stinky, nasty stuff
into his truck. While I've never had an opportunity to ask him about

his positive attitude, my guess is that he thinks very differently about his role than some might automatically assume. Does he see himself as someone who picks up other people's refuse? Or does he view himself as someone who protects people from disease...or takes care of his family...or does something vitally important for others?

Love and Logic Experiment

If you've never thought about it before, ask yourself, "What higher meaning or purpose can I attach to my job? What part of my daily work helps humankind?"

Finding purpose in our lives and occupations is the first step in most effectively helping our children find purpose in their lives...and school.

Can you *really* help your children develop a sense of purpose?

Absolutely! Like any other attitude or aptitude, a sense of purpose can be transmitted to your children through the three *E*'s of the Love and Logic approach.

The First *E* Stands for Example.

As we all know, children learn many of their most important life lessons by watching others in their lives. Albert Bandura, the father of Social Learning Theory, observed that children are most likely to emulate others they view as powerful and loving. As powerful and loving people in children's lives, are we modeling an attitude of purpose and servitude...or are we neglecting to take this immensely powerful teaching tool?

As I mentioned earlier, much of this modeling has to do with what children overhear us say. I was a very fortunate child in that I grew up hearing that my dad "gets to go to work" each day…rather than "has to go to work" each day. I was blessed to hear that both of my parents "got to learn new things" rather than "had to learn new things." What a difference one word made in my life!

My dad went to work each day to "help people." I'm not sure how many million times I heard him say that. As I grew, I began to think, "Someday I'm going to be lucky enough to work and help people!" Now I feel like one of the most fortunate people in the world!

I was also blessed to hear my parents talk about other adults in this way. They never talked down about people who made their living picking up cigarette butts, flipping hamburgers, crawling around under greasy cars, etc. We were taught that everybody is important and everybody has an important role in making the world a good and safe place to live.

Love and Logic Experiment

Children learn from our example, and they can learn from the example of other adults, too. Experiment with making a habit out of asking your children to describe what they believe to be the purpose others fulfill in your community. For example, you might ask them this as you are driving and spot workers performing road repairs.

When your child says something like:

They are fixing the street.

Reply with something like:

Yes, they are. And they are helping all of us by keeping the roads safe!

Are your kids overhearing you talking about your purpose? Do they see you doing things that serve others? In what sorts of things do they see you investing the lion's share of your time and energy? Are you all about yourself, or are you willing to share?

As I ask these questions, I recognize that I've have fallen short in this area. It's always simpler to write about such matters than to put them into practice each and every day! It's worth the effort, nevertheless, to keep on pressing toward the goal of being better and better. One of the most dramatic ways of doing this is to walk the talk by volunteering with your children.

Love and Logic Experiment

Make certain that your children see you volunteering. Even better, get them involved by your side. As a general rule, the act of working together toward the welfare of others serves as incredibly powerful medicine for whatever ails your child… and your relationship with your child. The challenge is to avoid letting your child's initial reaction to the prospect of volunteering deter you from getting them involved. Most children are unhappy at first yet grow to feel better and better as time goes by. Just keep doing it.

Such activities should never be entered into with the goal of punishing your child or teaching them a lesson. Instead, your heart condition must be one of sincere compassion for those in need, as well as a sincere desire to share this expression of love with your child.

The Second *E* of the Love and Logic Approach Stands for Experience.

Are your kids regularly involved in experiences that force them to place the needs and desires of others in front of their own? The best place to start with this is by making sure that they are contributing to the family by doing chores without reminders and without pay. In chapter four, I discussed the fact that chores are far more important than homework. Why? Simply because they serve as the first and most basic experience requiring delayed gratification, persistence, respect for authority, and selflessness as they enter into this challenging world. Those who are deprived of doing chores are deprived of the core competencies required for success in school and life:

> *If we can't get our kids to do chores at home,*
> *we should never expect their teachers*
> *to be capable of motivating them to do*
> *their schoolwork at school.*

I'd rather be irritatingly redundant than fail to emphasize the critical importance of chores in our children's lives. They really are that important! That's why I've included the quick tips below as a reminder of how we might "encourage" even the most difficult youngster to complete them.

• **A** stands for "**A**sk your child to do a chore you are sure they will either forget or refuse to do." Don't say, "Do it now!" Give them a deadline, instead: "Just have the vacuuming done by tomorrow afternoon at three." The deadline gives you plenty of time to think and plan if your child gets resistant.

- **B** stands for "**B**e quiet." Resist the urge to nag and remind. Just hope and pray that your child will not do the chore…so that they have a significant learning experience.

- **C** stands for "**C**onsequences and empathy will do the teaching." If your child forgets or refuses to do the chore, one option is to do it for them and expect them to pay you for your time and effort. Kids can "pay" in many different ways, including cash, collateral (toys or possessions), or doing without some of the luxuries you typically provide.

Listen to our CD titled *Didn't I Tell You to Take out the Trash?* for more ideas about getting kids to do chores without resorting to nagging, begging, or bribing.

Perhaps I understated something I mentioned just a bit earlier… the bit about volunteering with our children. Children must have the experience of volunteering in their communities. Yes! I used the word "must." Now I feel a bit better. This experience must also go beyond seeing us do it. They must be actively involved!

Over the past twenty-five years I've met thousands and thousands of youngsters. The ones who've really stood out in the crowd were those who spent a significant amount of time and energy volunteering. The maturity, confidence, and self-esteem radiated by these young people provide testimony to the critical importance of the need for purpose. And, by the way, these youngsters were typically the ones who also performed best in school!

Do your children know how much you value their involvement in helping others? Do they understand that this goes beyond organized volunteer activities? Do they see how even small acts of kindness contribute to a sense of purpose?

Love and Logic Experiment

Like anything else, our focus on providing children with the gift of purpose can fade over time. That's why it's helpful to develop some family traditions that keep it ever present in our minds… and our children's. One example involves developing a simple dinner table ritual where family members are encouraged to share examples of how they helped others during the day.

Of course, it's helpful if the adults go first by describing how they have served. This increases the likelihood that the children will as well.

Don't make the mistake of thinking that the examples have to be huge and impressive. Simple things like holding a door open for someone, helping another child who was being bullied at school, smiling and greeting an elderly neighbor, etc., are all small yet wonderful examples.

The goal is to establish a family identity heavily anchored by a sense of purpose extending beyond one's own desires.

Now…let's get real. As any reasonably experienced parent understands, getting kids to think and act beyond their own desires isn't always a piece of cake. What does a parent do when their youngsters act selfishly?

Rejoice!

Huh? What? Why in the world might a parent be joyful over the fact that their child is acting in self-centered ways? Joy can be had because this unkind behavior represents a marvelous mistake… a wonderful blunder capable of leading the child toward a great life lesson.

Have I already mentioned anything about small mistakes being good? Have I already discussed how we ought to pray for them… so that our young'uns learn when the price tags are still small?

As you know, the second *E* of the Love and Logic approach stands for experience. Sometimes our children need to experience some sad consequences for acting selfishly before they are willing to act *selflessly* and experience the happy feelings associated with helping.

When my children act selfishly, it really drains my energy. It really and truly leaves me feeling tired and sad. The great thing about this is that it provides the opportunity for me to have them replace these depleted ergs of energy by doing my chores, staying home instead of having me drive them somewhere they want to go, doing without something they want me to do…so that I can rest on the couch, selling some of their stuff so they can hire a babysitter…and their mom and I can go out to dinner without them, etc.

Have you ever heard that consequences must be logical? Have you ever heard that they should "fit" the crime? Yes indeed, the most effective consequences are the ones that have some logical connection to the misbehavior.

> *Having a child pay for a window they broke*
> *makes logical sense.*
> *Grounding a child for breaking*
> *a window doesn't.*

The problem as I see it is that most cases aren't so clear cut! Have you ever found yourself at a total and complete loss for a logical…legal…consequence? You're not alone. In such cases I recommend applying the Love and Logic Generic Consequence (AKA "The Energy Drain"). Over thirty years ago, the founders of the

Love and Logic Institute began to reason that it made logical sense for children to replace any parental energy drained by their bad decisions or bad behavior. Since that time, we've heard thousands of testimonials describing the simplicity and power of this approach. One father relayed this example:

> *We have been doing the Energy Drain since our daughter was four. Every time we couldn't think of a consequence, we would say, "Oh no. That really drains our energy." Then we would ask her how she planned to replace it. We helped her decide by giving her some ideas like dusting the baseboards, picking up sticks out in the yard, staying in her room so that we could rest, and other things. We still use it and she is twelve. The other day, she was being really snotty about helping her grandparents with some things. As soon as I said, "Oh, no, this really drains my energy," she started getting really busy helping her grandpa. The last thing she wants to do is a bunch of our chores to put our energy back!*

When your children fall into the habit of acting selfishly, might it be wise to let them experience relatively small consequences now…rather than the big ones they'll experience later on if they become selfish adults?

Love and Logic Experiment

The next time your child refuses to help, refuses to share, or develops a really bad attitude about doing so, experiment with informing them that they have just drained your energy.

Don't feel like you need to explain this at that precise moment. Just give yourself some time to think about how they might

---

replace your energy. In the meantime, simply allow your child to think you are very strange…and to think that they have gotten away with the bad behavior. Go to them later and ask:

How are you planning to replace the energy you drained by refusing to help?

When they act like you're from another planet give them some options like the following:

• *Some kids decide to do some of my chores.*
• *Some kids decide to sell some of their stuff so that they can buy me a gift certificate to the spa.*
• *Some kids decide to get nasty and wait to see if their parents are really serious about this.*

Wish them luck, and give them a reasonable deadline for replacing your energy.

Resist the urge to nag, remind, or warn. Simply hope that they forget so that they experience a "double learning experience." If they fail to replace your energy, you may have go to Plan B…which involves saying the following any time they want you to cook them something they like, wash their favorite clothes, drive them some-where, buy them the goodies they like to eat, etc.:

Oh. This is so sad. I do extra things for kids who have a good attitude about helping and replace my energy when they drain it.

Of course, doing this with empathy will make the dif-ference between your children learning responsibility versus learning resentment.

NOTHING WORKS WITHOUT THE EMPATHY.

The Third *E* of the Love and Logic Approach Stands for Empathy.

I can remember my father before he and Dr. Foster Cline developed the Love and Logic way. He was a great dad…but a pretty loud and kind of angry-acting one when anything went wrong. He also seemed tired all of the time.

In the mid 1970s, he and Dr. Cline began to notice that there was a certain subset of parents and educators who were naturals at raising respectful and responsible kids. After close observation and study, they realized that the common denominator among these natural greats was their expression of genuine empathy when kids made mistakes and experienced the related consequences.

As he began to internalize the importance of empathy and began to use it more frequently, our relationship really blossomed. I began to realize how much he loved me and how much he wanted the best for me. I also noticed that he wasn't so tired all of the time!

When children really see how much we love them and our sadness that they have to learn from mistakes by experiencing some consequences, they're far more likely to learn from their mistakes… instead of blaming us for their discomfort. We also enjoy the freedom of knowing that the weight of the world is no longer resting on our shoulders. We begin to realize that we can allow consequences to do the teaching…instead of feeling like we have to use anger, lectures, or threats to get the job done. What a relief!

Another beautiful benefit of empathy involves the vicarious learning that takes place.

Every time we use empathy we teach empathy.

Are your children learning an empathetic attitude toward others, or are they coming to believe that they should pass judgment on others who are less fortunate? Do they feel empathy for others who've made poor decisions, or do they think, "That's what you get when you do stupid things like that."?

Can you see how our use of empathy with our kids can lead them toward having a more humble...and graceful...attitude toward others? On the flip side, can you also see how the use of anger, sarcasm, or criticism can have the opposite effect?

As you can imagine, children who lack empathy for others find it completely impossible to develop a sense of purpose that goes beyond simply meeting their own needs and desires. In contrast, those who feel empathy for the less fortunate are far more likely to be motivated by a heartfelt desire to improve the human condition.

Which child will remain more motivated in school when the going gets tough?

During my days in psychology graduate school I met another student named Dave. More passionate about learning than the rest of us combined, he worked his fingers to the bone studying, writing, and volunteering at a local hospital. Somewhat envious of his energy and drive, I asked him how he managed to burn the candle at both ends without getting burned. I'll never forget his humble answer:

My mom died of cancer when I was in elementary school. During her sickness and all of her treatments I could tell how scared she was. The day she passed away I said to myself, "Someday I'm going to help people who are dying. Someday I'm going to help them feel not-so-scared."

Dave's story reminds us that there is nothing more motivating than a sense of purpose. While he developed his purpose through great personal tragedy, our children don't have to. We can take the lead in our families and show them how to enjoy the tremendous benefits of benefiting others.

Loving Our Kids for Who They Are

Children who are loved for who they are experience the freedom to become the best that they can be.

Our Dreams

I think it's safe to say that all of us harbor dreams about how our kids are going to turn out. Let's spy on a young couple as they entertain high hopes about their firstborn son. Can you see them? That's right! Their house is the second one on the left...the white one with a front porch. There they are, swaying to and fro on their porch swing:

Patting her pregnant belly, Mrs. Normal coos, "Ahh… isn't he going to be amazing?"

Mr. Normal smiles at the starry sky and replies, "Yeah...I can't wait to look into his eyes for the first time."

Snuggling her hubby, Mrs. N. adds, "And I can see him right now...sitting at in-school suspension because he's refused to do his math worksheets."

*Nodding, Mr. N. coos, "Yep. I can see him, too. And...won't it
be great if he qualifies for special education services?"*

While it's normal to have dreams for our offspring, those entertained
by Mr. and Mrs. Normal...well...they ain't so normal! More typically,
we hope and dream for healthy, happy, highly responsible kids who
do well in school, have plenty of friends, and never end up with
their pictures hanging in the post office. Our dreams are for Penn
State...not the state pen!

These dreams begin far before the youngster they're attached to
takes her first breath. They roll around in our heads far before we
hear her first cry...or hold her in our arms...or gaze into her eyes.
Our dreams are born first...then comes our child.

Since our hopes and dreams represent the first "experience" we
have with our children, they tend to become as real in our hearts
and minds as the precious flesh and blood that follows. In essence,
almost every child is born with a twin...not an identical one...but
an intensely loved one residing within his parents' minds.

When Reality Doesn't Match the Dream

Ten-year-old Ray was a wonderful child with all the makings of a
super-duper adult. He was a good reader, liked to play his trumpet,
made friends like a champ, and even knew how to catch grasshop-
pers without them slipping between his fingers. He was a great
kid...who refused to do a darn thing in school.

Ray's parents were great people, too! Worried deeply about Ray's
refusal to do anything even remotely academic, they asked me to
spend some time getting to know him. "Maybe," they thought, "this
psychologist might be able to figure out why Ray is so reluctant."

As Ray's trust in me developed, he began to relay more and more sadness, low self-esteem…and loneliness. He missed his parents. He missed their love, their attention, and their encouragement. He resented the fact that they spent all of their time and energy on his brother, Tim. He hated the fact that all they could think about was Tim. He hated the fact that Tim was always more important. He hated the fact that it seemed he'd never measure up to Tim. Because of this, Ray spent most of his time trying to be the exact opposite of Tim…an underachiever!

When I first met Ray, his brother, Tim, had been dead for almost two years. His parents…normal, loving people…were so enveloped by grief and loss that nothing else existed. The wonderful son they still had was eclipsed by the son they once had.

Elizabeth Kubler-Ross, in her classic book *On Death and Dying*, described the process through which people must progress as they come to grips with their own terminal illness or the loss of a loved one. The end stage of healthy acceptance and peace comes only through successful navigation of the earlier stages listed below:

DENIAL:	"This isn't happening."
ANGER:	"Somebody needs to pay for this!"
BARGAINING:	"There's got to be some way to make this all go away."
DEPRESSION:	"There's no point in going on. There's no hope."

The unimaginable pain associated with the death of a child was keeping Ray's parents from demonstrating their never-ending love for him. As the months and years went by, this pain never disappeared, but it yielded a spot in their hearts for the love they had for their living son. Learning how much Ray needed them to focus on his needs helped them remember what a joyous blessing he was. This gave them a renewed purpose and the strength to move toward acceptance. Ray was no longer a sad, depressed child living in the shadows.

My heart goes out to those of you who've lost a child. I pray that the pain in your heart will allow a space for love to reenter. I pray that you will find peace and renewed joy in those who love you.

Now...some of you may be wondering, "What does Ray's story have to do with me? I've never experienced the pain of losing a child."

Does Ray's example remind you of how precious your children really are? Does it remind you of how blessed you are?

While you may not be grieving the loss of a child, is it even remotely possible that you are grieving the loss of a dream child... one conceived in your mind long before your real flesh and blood entered this world? Is it even remotely possible that this grief is making it more difficult for you to totally and completely love your child for who she is...not what you want her to become?

Christina, like Ray, was a sad, lonely, and apathetic child. Like so many others I've met, her deceased dream twin consumed the lion's share of her parents' emotional energy. Never in her wildest dreams could she ever imagine measuring up to the memory of this perfectly-behaved, high-achieving sibling. The prospects of such seemed overwhelming. "Far less threatening," Christina reasoned, "to become her late twin's alter ego." Far better," she thought, "to be the black sheep...to be the rebel...to act like I don't care."

While nothing can ever compare to the pain of losing a real flesh and blood child, the death of our dreams...no matter how unrealistic they might have been...results in the very same, albeit far less intense...grief process. Denial is not a river in Egypt! While navigating this stage, our attentions are drawn toward how wrong everyone else is about our child's unique strengths and weaknesses. With one of my sons I was convinced that he would be the rough and tumble, throw-caution-to-the-wind sort of mountain boy that I was. As truth would have it, he was born a very sensitive, rather anxious chap who'd rather stay inside and draw than go outside and climb pine trees. I wasted far too much energy parenting my dream...not my child.

Because of this, I also spent too much time being frustrated with him, trying to coax him into being Daniel Boone, and being rather depressed about the fact that he might never feel the urge to brave the elements in search of adventure. It wasn't until I really came to grips with the fact that God makes all children different... and beautiful...that I realized that I was missing out on the wonderful little guy he was.

Too frequently parents come to this state of awareness after they have so severely damaged their relationship with their child that it takes a lifetime to repair it. Because their dream is for an academically talented one...or an athletic one...or a musically skilled one...etc... they fail to recognize that the child they do have has significant gifts in other areas. Making matters even tougher, our society and many of our schools send the message that children cannot possibly become successful adults unless they excel in academics.

Slamming the Door to Success

Imagine the following scenario:

> *After a long and very difficult day of work, you hop in your car and head home. While driving, your mind drifts off to how won-derful life will be when you walk through the front door and see*

your loving spouse. He'll be there to greet you with a smile. He'll be there to hold you in his arms. He'll be there to listen as you vent about how ridiculously clueless and unfair your boss has been.

As you drive into the driveway a smile appears on your face as you anticipate his love. Walking through the front door, you hear his voice, "Honey? Is that you?"

Without hesitation you begin to share your day, "You aren't going to believe the day I had today. My boss…"

It doesn't take long for you to sense that something is wrong. He's not listening.

"Sweetie," he replies, "I can imagine what happened today, because I talked to your boss and heard about how you haven't been applying yourself at work. You have so much potential, but you just don't want to put in the work required for you to reach it."

"But uh, but he…" is all you can muster.

Your loving spouse pats you on the back and produces what looks like some sort of carefully constructed and rather complex chart. "If you bring your work home with you," he urges, "then we can go over it together, and you can redo it until it's correct. That's why I spent the day making this chart."

Ignoring the disappointment and sadness written all over your face, he continues, "For example, if you bring your work home with you on Monday…and work with me on your skill deficiencies…guess what you get to put right here? I went down to the teacher supply store. Do you know that they have all sorts of really neat stickers? These are scratch and sniff!"

You're no longer disappointed and sad. Now you're mad…really, really mad! "This is the stupidest thing I…"

"See…that's the attitude!" he interrupts. "That's the attitude you get anytime somebody tries to help you. I love you, and I

know that you have so much potential as an employee…and a spouse! If you would just get a better attitude…then you wouldn't be so stressed every day. Besides, if you get at least four stickers per week, I'll take you to Pizza Palace!"

Some questions to ponder:
- What are the odds that your spouse's well-intentioned plan will leave you highly motivated to work on your skill deficiencies?
- Will you be highly motivated to work toward enough scratch and sniff stickers to earn a trip to pepperoni paradise at Pizza Palace?
- What sort of effect will your spouse's lovingly conceived plan have on the level of emotional intimacy in your marriage?
- Is there any chance that you're now feeling like your spouse only loves you when you're producing?
- Is there any possibility that you feel put down by your spouse… that you feel like he thinks you're stupid?
- Do we ever attempt similar approaches with our kids?
- Is it possible that they feel pretty much the same way you felt when your spouse described his plan?
- Is there any better way to demoralize and demotivate the people we love than to give them this sort of "help"?

Opening the Door to Success

Let's press "REWIND," go back to the beginning, and see if a different approach might leave you feeling more hopeful about work…and your marriage:

After a long and very difficult day of work, you hop in your car and head home. While driving, your mind drifts off to how wonderful life will be when you walk through the front door and see your loving spouse. He'll be there to greet you with a smile. He'll be there to hold you in his arms. He'll be there to listen as you vent about how ridiculously clueless and unfair your boss has been.

As you drive into the driveway a smile appears on your face as you anticipate his love. Walking through the front door, you hear his voice, "Honey? Is that you?"

Without hesitation you begin to share your day, "You aren't going to believe the day I had today. My boss…"

It doesn't take long before you remember why you married this man. He looks into your eyes and he does a very, very wise thing: He resists the urge to deploy the roll of duct tape hanging from his belt. He resists his instinct to come to the rescue with a quick fix. Instead, he looks into your eyes and says, "Frustrating."

You agree, "Yes! And you know what else he did…"

As you catch your breath, he replies, "Upsetting." You agree with that, too. "Yes! Your boss IS completely clueless." As you take another breath, he hugs you and adds, "I love you. I wish I could help."

How's he doing?
- Would this second scenario go a bit further toward bringing the best out of you?
- Is it possible that your spouse's love might just leave you more motivated to make the best out of your job?
- What will best motivate your children to do well in school? Will it be a chart that keeps track of how much homework they are doing? Will it be some well-worn lectures about how much better they will do if they apply themselves? Or…might it be the uncon-ditional, never-ending love and empathy they receive when they

make mistakes, blow tests, get bad reports, or encounter tough teachers and tough subjects?

• Have you noticed that really, really effective people use very few words when those around them are upset?

To a significant extent, the answer to the problem of underachievement lies right in front of our noses, too close to be seen by many. It's not a complex or highly technical solution. It's a solution that opens the door for achievement by convincing kids that we love and value them for who they are today...not what we want them to become tomorrow. It's a solution requiring that we become the special people in their lives who make it safe to take healthy risks, safe to look silly, safe to blunder, and safe to excel. It's a solution that requires letting go of our dreams and really loving and accepting our flesh and blood children.

Ten Ways to Help Your Kids Feel Loved

I know that you love your kids! Why am I so sure? Parents who care very little for their children don't read books like this one. They definitely don't make it to the final chapter!

Sadly, I've worked with scores of children who were unconditionally loved by their parents yet didn't perceive this to be the case. Much to their parents' dismay, these youngsters truly believed that they would never measure up.

Anyone who's been married for more than one day knows that the messages we intend to send aren't always the ones received! That's why I close this book with ten intentional ways of demonstrating how head-over-heels in love you are with your kids. All of these tips are time-tested. All of them go far beyond simple words…to the actions and unstated messages that demonstrate true love. All of them are designed to get below the surface…to get at the heart of what leaves others feeling loved, secure, and motivated.

Number One

Remember that each and every child is conceived as a uniquely gifted individual.

The internet is rife with "informative" articles from "experts" indicating what sorts of academic skills our youngsters should master by the time they reach certain ages. Information from some of these sources may be helpful to provide a very general sense of whether young children are experiencing any sort of severe developmental lags in need of remediation.

Nevertheless, wise parents possess a healthy distrust about everything they read on the internet. (Except, of course, what they read on loveandlogic.com!) Smart folks don't make major life decisions based on what they've read on the internet! Instead, they take this information and they compare it with information received from other sources, including their child's pediatrician, her teachers, a trusted counselor, etc. If concerned, they ask, "Is my child's development falling within the *broad range* of what's considered *normal* for her age?"

"Broad" and "range" are two of the most important words we can remember about raising kids…and loving them for the uniquely gifted people they are. Where some internet sites and blogs become potentially destructive is when people begin to prescribe very narrow requirements for what our children should be doing by certain ages. Combine this misinformation with the opinions of friends and relatives…as well as the bragging of other parents…and we have fertile soil for the growth of fear and dissatisfaction with our child's unique and beautiful nature.

Please forgive me for being redundant…but I simply cannot stress this point strongly enough. Every child is uniquely gifted. Each of your children is uniquely gifted! A marvelous thing happens when we become passionate about identifying our youngsters' special blessings: We begin to let go of self-blame, guilt, and embarrassment. We begin to let go of the frustration. We begin to fall even more deeply in love with our kids. We begin to communicate the messages that leave them perceiving the same level of love that we've always felt for them in our hearts.

Number Two

Avoid "constructive criticism."

Have you ever had the displeasure of being around someone who believed in "constructive criticism"? Oh the joy! The words "constructive" and "criticism" fit together about as logically as "bureaucratic" and "efficiency"… or "jumbo" and "shrimp." Very few of us find ourselves being drawn toward critical folks whose life passion is to identify what we are doing wrong so that they can lead us toward more "constructive" behavior. Maybe I'm just strange or exceptionally strong-willed, but I find it more gratifying to do things WRONG than to be around people who are dead set on setting me straight.

When it comes to their children, many extremely loving people convey very subtle, yet extremely demotivating types of criticism. Without raising their voices, or coming across in any sort of sarcastic or angry way, they leave their kids feeling like they never measure up.

They do this by:

- Spending most of their time trying to make sure that their kids always do their schoolwork correctly.
- Being afraid to let their children experiment with doing things differently…or incorrectly… and learning from the natural consequences of their actions.
- Being fearful that their children are not smart enough to learn from these consequences.

All of these actions culminate in our kids feeling criticized. This doesn't mean that we've *intended* for them to feel this way. It simply means that this is the way many children perceive it.

What a gift you can give your children…and yourself…by allowing them to learn from the real world rather than your "constructive" criticism.

Number Three

Avoid critical talk about others.

Since it's unlikely that you're like me and occasionally find yourself focusing on the faults of others, I hesitate to mention this one. Well…just in case you are like me and do slip into this, remember the following:

> *When our children overhear us*
> *being critical of others*
> *it doesn't take long for them to wonder*
> *if they are next on our list.*

In contrast, when they overhear us focusing on the assets of others, they become far less fearful to take the sorts of healthy risks required to learn and grow. They're also far more likely to develop patient and positive attitudes toward others.

Number Four

Avoid saying, "Try it. It's easy!"

Have you ever had someone say this to you…and found out pretty quickly that the task you'd been coaxed into attempting was painfully difficult? Did this leave you feeling exceptionally capable…or downright stupid and embarrassed?

How many times does this have to happen to our children before they feel like they can't measure up?

Very frequently well-meaning parents and educators use this phrase in an attempt to urge a reluctant child into trying something they're afraid of. When the child finds the task easy, all is right with the world. When they don't, they're confronted with the pain of seeing that they might be so slow that they can't even do something easy!

How many times does this have to happen before a child is completely unwilling to try anything difficult?

A far more effective approach involves saying the following:

A lot of kids find this kind of challenging.
Would you try this and let me know what you think?

If your child replies, "It's too hard. I can't do it," experiment with smiling, patting them on the back, and asking:

Aren't you glad that I don't believe that?

You might also add:

The good thing is that I'm going to love you the same even if you have to work really hard to figure this out.

Number Five

Notice and describe instead of praising.

If you're taking the time to read this book, the odds are extremely high that you want your children to believe that you love them. Something that can get in the way of this message is the constant use of praise when they succeed.

If you've been led to believe that praise is always a good thing, you're not alone! Many popular psychology books have led us astray by suggesting that we ought to run around all day gushing over our kids with "Wow! That's great!" or "You are so smart!" or "Great job!" While a small measure of this is good, too much can create major problems.

The very first thing we ought to establish here is what I mean by "praise." Praise involves providing any sort of positive yet nonspecific feedback. Examples include:

• Great work!
• Wow!
• That's awesome!
• Super!

One problem with praise is that it fails to give our children specific feedback about what they've achieved that qualifies as being so great or special. This leaves many of them wondering, "Is this person really sincere, or are they just trying to get me to do what they want?"

Praise also places emphasis on results rather than effort and perseverance. Quite frankly many tasks required for success in life require sustained hard work, resulting in less than exciting short-term results. Excessive praise leads children (and some politicians) to believe that performing such duties…or taking such risks… never pays off. In essence they come to believe:

> *It's far wiser to do easier things that guarantee the praise of others than to attempt more difficult things that might result in struggle or failure.*

Excess praise creates kids who take the safe route. It also creates kids who fear that they won't be loved as much if they fail.

Number Six

Focus on their strains…not their brains.

One of the many downfalls of applying excessive praise involves the potential message it sends about the root cause of success in academics…or just about anything else in life.

The only cause of success with human control involves the amount of effort or strain we are willing to invest in a given task. People who understand this are people who are far more willing to work hard and persevere when the going gets tough. They're also the folks far more willing to pick themselves back up and try again when they make mistakes or experience discouraging setbacks.

As I mentioned in chapter two, our children are far more likely to develop success-oriented attitudes when we help them focus on effort as the key to success rather than good luck or intelligence. When we make a habit of saying things like, "You can do this! You are so smart!" or "Great job! You are so bright," we set them up for a fall when they encounter tasks they find challenging. Almost immediately, they begin to think, "Oh, I guess this isn't one of those things I'm bright enough to handle. I might as well give up."

When we spend too much time praising our children over how intelligent or "bright" they are we also run the risk of them believing that our love for them is conditional…dependent upon how intelligent or "bright" they are. This leads many children to take the safe route by avoiding any sort of task that may result in failure. Very sadly, this has also led many to give up on their parents' love by adopting a persona 180 degrees from their parents' ideal. Subconsciously they conclude, "It's less painful to be the black sheep than fail and look dumb to Mom and Dad."

The solution involves a simple emphasis on the effort and perseverance our children produce…rather than the number of neurons present between their ears. When we focus on their strains, the implicit message is that all we really want them to achieve is their very best effort. Listed below are some examples you can use with your kids:

• You worked really hard on that.
• You kept trying even though it was hard.
• You didn't give up.
• You really gave that your best effort.
• You did your best even though you knew it was going to be hard.

Go back to pages 19 and 20, and reread how you might supercharge this process.

Number Seven

Listen with acceptance.

From the passenger seat of my father's 1969 Chrysler Town and Country station wagon I proclaimed, "I don't know why everybody is so uptight about their kids getting good grades. It's not like you really need an education or anything like that. Besides, I can make plenty of money working at Village Inn."

I was sixteen. My dad was older and wiser and full of this new stuff called Love and Logic. That's why he didn't lose control of that big Chrysler by trying to reach over and strangle me. That's why he didn't lose control of himself by launching into a tired old tangent. Instead, he asked questions, listened with sincere interest, and dodged the control battle.

"That's an option," he remarked. "What do you like best about working at Village Inn?"

I replied, "You can drink all of the coffee you want and the people that work there are really cool."

With not a hint of sarcasm in his voice he replied, "That does sound nice. Is there anything else about it that you like?"

"Uh," I answered, "yeah…if you work on really busy nights and on Sunday you can make really good tips."

"Sounds like you feel pretty lucky to have that job," he continued with sincere interest. "Do they pay enough to cover rent, car insurance, utilities, and other expenses?"

A bit annoyed I replied, "Uh…well…yeah. You get raises after you work there longer!"

With great love in his voice, he said, "The great thing about you, Charlie, is that you've got what it takes to make good choices about your life. No matter what, your mom and I will love you."

Can you imagine how frustrated I was by his refusal to play? Can you imagine how irritated I was when he simply listened instead of trying to tell me what to do with my life? I wanted to see the veins in his forehead bulge! I wanted to see him turn red! That would have been fun and exciting. Then I could have shown him who was really in control by refusing to learn a thing at school!

Is it possible that his willingness to listen actually played a part in my willingness to get an education rather than spending my life fighting him by bussing tables?

The truth be told, most kids eventually test their parents to see if they've got the guts and wisdom to love instead of dictate. Loving means that we listen and accept their feelings and beliefs…even when their feelings and beliefs make us cringe. Dictating means that we try to lecture them into believing the way that we do. Loving means that we ask some questions that plant seeds about possible consequences. Dictating means that we try to scare them by telling them how bad things will turn out. Loving means realizing that they, ultimately, are the only ones who can determine the course of their lives. Dictating means trying to control them even when it's clear that we cannot. Loving means that we love them even when they make decisions we believe are unwise. Dictating implies that our love for them depends on whether they do what we want.

Loving doesn't mean that we'll simply stand by and let them behave horribly. Loving simply means understanding that they are far more likely to make good decisions when we aren't locking horns in unwinnable power struggles. Remember this the next time your child says something like, "I don't need an education. I'm going to be a professional skateboarder," or "School is so overrated. Kids who are into that stuff are just buying into the system."

Number Eight

Allow them to walk their own path.

Most of us probably have a path we'd *like* our kids to follow. Sometimes they share our sense of direction. Sometimes they invent their own type of compass.

My wife and I have very similar views of where we want to go in life. We also share very similar ideas about where to drive when we have the time to take a vacation road trip. That's where the similarities end!

I enjoy the back roads…the scenic route if you will. My wife likes highways because they get you there faster. I like to stop at truck stops and tacky tourist traps. She likes to pass them at the speed of light. I like to sip coffee and take plenty of bathroom breaks. She drinks nothing…so that she doesn't have to stop for bathroom breaks. While our approaches to land travel differ greatly, we love and enjoy each other because we have dedicated ourselves to learning how to avoid taking each other's travel preferences personally. Both of us are committed to remembering that our desired paths…or basic personalities…were largely determined before each of us took our first breath.

So is the case with our kids! Is it helpful to remember that they don't wake each morning and make a written plan for irritating us with their travel plans? Is it helpful to remember that they have a special path that is largely determined by their unique personalities…rather than their desire to ignore our wise counsel?

Please don't misunderstand! Not for a millisecond am I suggesting that we ought to stand by and simply watch our children self-destruct. Not for a millisecond am I encouraging you to sit idle as they damage themselves or others. What I am suggesting is that far too many children become discouraged and choose self-destructive paths because their parents have not allowed them to follow their unique and positive path. Can you imagine how much pain my wife and I would experience if we devoted each road trip to the remediation of each other's path preferences? I can! We've tried that before.

> *Loving others for who they are is the magic*
> *that allows them to achieve what they can become.*

Do you have an artistic, creative child who you've tried to make into an analytic, organized one? Do you have a sensitive, introspective child who you've tried to make into an extroverted one? Do you have an active, mechanically oriented child who you've tried to turn into a calm, introspective and focused one?

Number Nine

Take the time to play with them.

How simple. Just take time to play with them.

Is it *really* that simple? Yes…and…no.

Yes, the simple act of playing with our children does far more to boost their motivation to do well in school than all of the lectures ever given to all of the children who've ever walked the face of the earth! When we take the time to play with them…and to play what *they* want to play, we show them how deeply we love them.

When this happens, they're far more likely to identify with our values, including our educational ones.

When I consider the vast number of high achieving students I've known, one of the things that stands out in their lives is the amount of time their parents spent with them playing, participating in sports, or enjoying hobbies. These wise parents intuitively understood that "quality time" can't happen without "quantity time."

William's conscientious father was always quick to point out that he and his son enjoyed plenty of "quality time" together. Dad truly believed that the quality of this time made up for the lack of quantity. His son, William, never did. In fact, William never felt close to his father, and he never felt close to his father's values either.

William is a real person whom I know very well. William isn't the only child I've known who's grown up believing that he just wasn't important enough for his parents to spend much time with. William reminds me that the things I think are important...like having a clean car, having a perfect lawn, spending time with my buddies, etc...pale in importance to spending plenty of QUALITY time with my family.

"Quality time" can't happen without "quantity time."

The not-so-simple part of this comes into play when the survival of the family depends upon a parent working long hours. A loved and rather well-known preacher often comments on his experience being raised by a single mother who worked her fingers to the bone each and every day. Because he knew that she had no choice, her lack of time spent with him was not perceived as lack of love...but as necessity. Because she did her best, he perceived her many hours away from him as her expression of intense love…as a needed sacrifice that she was willing to make to take care of him.

When our children understand that we are doing our best in this regard, they understand that our best is done out of great love for them. In contrast, when they see that we're making excuses because our priorities are askew, they believe that they aren't very important to us.

Number Ten

Give them the gift of empathy.

My Great Aunt Genevieve had a favorite saying about relationships…

You don't really know a person until you eat a box of salt together.

For years I wondered what it must be like to eat a box of salt. Yuck! I also wondered what this had to do with knowing people. In desperation, I even turned to the internet for answers! No luck. Apparently there were no documented societal rituals involving the consumption of large quantities of sodium chloride with the purpose of knowing other folks on a higher level.

At the young age of 99, she finally explained it to me. Pulling me close and whispering in my ear, she explained, "You see, Charlie, you don't know what somebody is really like until you go through hard times together. Anybody can be sweet when everything is going good. Just wait till bad things happen. That's when ya get to see how they tick."

How simple, and how true!

What do your kids see when they bring home a box of salt in the form of a bad report card? What happens when that box of salt rears its ugly head as refusal to do their homework? What happens when that box of salt is represented by them forgetting to do their chores…or losing the coat you just bought them…or coming home late…or even crashing your car? What do they see from you when their overall attitude is box-o-salt-like?

Every time your child makes a poor decision, acts irresponsibly, or behaves disrespectfully, they give you a wonderful opportunity to show them who you really are…and how you love them more than they can ever imagine. Every time you take advantage of this opportunity with loving empathy, you also plant the seeds of joy for a lifetime.

NOTHING WORKS WITHOUT THE EMPATHY.

Thanks for reading!

Charles Fay, Ph.D.

Charles Fay, Ph.D. is a parent, author, and consultant to schools, parent groups, and mental health professionals around the world. His expertise in developing and teaching practical discipline strategies has been refined through work with severely disturbed youth in school, hospital, and community settings. Charles has developed an acute understanding of the most challenging students. Having grown up with Love and Logic, he also provides a unique...and often humorous...perspective.

Index